Instructor's Manual and Test Bank to Accompany

FIFTH EDITION

TEN STEPS *to* BUILDING COLLEGE READING SKILLS

John Langan

ATLANTIC CAPE COMMUNITY COLLEGE

Books in the Townsend Press Reading Series:

Groundwork for College Reading with Phonics
Groundwork for College Reading
Ten Steps to Building College Reading Skills
Ten Steps to Improving College Reading Skills
Ten Steps to Advancing College Reading Skills
Ten Steps to Advanced Reading

Books in the Townsend Press Vocabulary Series:

Vocabulary Basics
Groundwork for a Better Vocabulary
Building Vocabulary Skills
Building Vocabulary Skills, Short Version
Improving Vocabulary Skills
Improving Vocabulary Skills, Short Version
Advancing Vocabulary Skills
Advancing Vocabulary Skills, Short Version
Advanced Word Power

Supplements Available for Most Books:

Instructor's Edition
Instructor's Manual and Test Bank
Online Exercises
PowerPoint Presentations
Blackboard Cartridges

Printed in the United States of America
9 8 7 6 5 4 3 2 1

ISBN-13: 978-1-59194-246-7
ISBN-10: 1-59194-246-2

For book orders and requests for desk copies or supplements, contact us in any of the following ways:

By telephone: 1-800-772-6410
By fax: 1-800-225-8894
By e-mail: cs@townsendpress.com
Through our website: www.townsendpress.com

CONTENTS

Notes:

1. There are four mastery tests for each skill, supplementing the six mastery tests in the book itself. These tests can be used at a variety of points along the student's path of working through the chapter and the mastery tests in the book.

*2. These tests are identical to the Alternate Mastery Tests for this text available at the TP Online Learning Center (**www.townsendpress.net**). Instructors therefore have the option of assigning them either in print format or electronically.*

NOTES FOR INSTRUCTORS

On the first three pages of the Instructor's Edition of *Ten Steps to Building College Reading Skills*, Fifth Edition, I list some hints for teaching a reading course and for using the book. I add here some other comments.

Using a Class Contract

In the first class of the semester, I explain to students that I regard the course as a serious, professional relationship between them and me. I say that I want them to sign a professional contract for taking the course. I then pass out a contract for them to read and sign.

In my experience, the contract helps motivate younger students in particular to come to class and to assume responsibility for their own learning. Some of the older students don't need such a contract, but they welcome a clear presentation of basic ground rules regarding attendance and grading in the course.

A copy of the contract appears on pages 6–7; you have permission to modify and use this contract in whatever way you see fit.

Supplements for the Book

There are five supplements for the book:

- An *Instructor's Edition,* which is identical to the student book except that it provides the answers to all of the practices and tests.
- The combined *Instructor's Manual and Test Bank,* which you are now reading.
- *Online exercises* consisting of two additional mastery tests for each skill plus two combined-skills tests—22 tests in all. Instructors may also make additional online mastery tests available. These tests are free for students and instructors using the book and may be accessed at the Online Learning Center area of **www.townsendpress.com**.
- *PowerPoint slides* and *Blackboard cartridges*, available in the "Supplements" area for instructors at **www.townsendpress.com**.

If you've adopted *Ten Steps to Building College Reading Skills* for use in your reading classes, you're entitled to free copies of the two print supplements. Call 1-800-772-6410 or e-mail us at **cs@townsendpress.com** to get them shipped out to you immediately.

A Suggested Syllabus

Weeks 1–10:

One way to begin using the book is to have students work through the activities in "How to Become a Better Reader and Thinker" on pages 25–31. Then, as the first homework assignment, ask them to read "Getting Off to a Strong Start" on pages 3–13 and the essay "One Reader's Story" on pages 15–24, and urge them to take advantage of the book offer on pages 12–13. In the next class, discuss the questions on page 24; you may wish to ask students to write a paper on one of the questions as well.

I suggest then teaching one chapter from Part One a week, following the order in the book. Generally, at the end of a chapter, I give two tests: one for practice and one that counts for a grade.

I go over the tests in class right after students take them. (I recommend collecting test papers as students finish and distributing them to students in other parts of the room. Some students resist putting X's on a paper that belongs to the person sitting right next to them.) That way, students get immediate feedback on how they have done. Also, after class all I need to do is to check the grades quickly and transfer them to my grade book.

As the semester progresses, I use additional mastery tests, every so often, to review previous skills covered in the class.

Weeks 11–15:

In the last five weeks, students read two selections a week from Part Two of the book. They also do the remaining mastery tests, including some of the tests in this manual, as well as the combined-skills tests in the book and in this manual.

Having done all of the reading of the materials in the book, as well as all of the thinking required to complete the many activities, students are, in my experience, better readers and thinkers. They are better equipped both to handle a standardized reading test at the semester's end and to go on to content courses in their college curriculum.

Suggested Answers to the Discussion Questions

Pages 23–42 in this manual provide suggested answers to the discussion questions that follow each of the twenty readings in Parts One and Two of the book. There was simply no room in the Instructor's Edition for this material.

Writing Assignments

Writing and reading are closely related skills: practice at one will make a student better at the other. Also, writing about a selection is an excellent way of thinking about it. For these reasons, two writing assignments are provided (beginning on page 588 of the book) for each of the twenty reading selections in Parts One and Two.

If you ask students to write about a selection, I suggest you first have them read the "Brief Guide to Effective Writing" that appears on pages 586–587.

Teaching Vocabulary

One basic change that I've made in my teaching of reading is that I now directly teach vocabulary. We all know that students don't know enough words. Because they don't, they have trouble understanding what they read, and they're limited in what they can write. (We have all seen how, in standardized reading tests, students are frustrated because they don't know enough of the words in a passage to understand it and to answer comprehension questions about it. And we all know that because of the vocabulary problem, the standardized tests that are intended to measure reading comprehension are often in fact serving as vocabulary tests.)

I teach vocabulary using a words-in-context approach. (It is of no value to ask students to memorize isolated lists of vocabulary words.) Specifically, I use a book titled *Building Vocabulary Skills, Short Version*, by Sherrie Nist. There are twenty chapters in this book, with ten words in each chapter. I do the first chapter in class, so that students learn how to use the pronunciation key for the words and understand just how the chapter works. I then assign one or two chapters a week for homework.

In class each week, I walk around and check students' books to see that they have worked through the four pages of material for each chapter. (After this quick check, I then return the focus of the class to reading skills.) Every third week, I give students one of the several tests that follow each unit of five chapters in the book. My vocabulary syllabus looks like this:

Week 2: Vocabulary chapter 1 covered in class
Week 3: Vocabulary chapters 2–3 for homework
Week 4: Vocabulary chapters 4–5 for homework plus a test on Unit One in class
Week 5: Vocabulary chapters 6–7 for homework
Week 6: Vocabulary chapters 8–9 for homework
Week 7: Vocabulary chapter 10 for homework plus a test on Unit Two in class
Week 8: Vocabulary chapters 11–12 for homework
Week 9: Vocabulary chapters 13–14 for homework
Week 10: Vocabulary chapter 15 for homework plus a test on Unit Three in class
Week 11: Vocabulary chapters 16–17 for homework
Week 12: Vocabulary chapters 18–19 for homework
Week 13: Vocabulary chapter 20 for homework plus a test on Unit Four in class

The Importance of Continual Reading and Thinking

Continual reading—coupled with thinking about what one has read—is the very heart of a reading class. *One improves the skills of reading and thinking by guided reading and thinking.* This statement is emphasized with good reason. If a teacher is not careful, he or she may play too participatory a role in the classroom, getting more reading and thinking practice than the student does. The teacher should serve as a manager, using the materials in the text to give students the skills practice they need. *Ten Steps to Building College Reading Skills* helps the teacher ensure that students do a great deal of active reading and thinking in the classroom.

The Importance of Constant Feedback

Along with continual reading, writing, and thinking, it is vital that students get frequent feedback. Here are ways they can secure such feedback:

- Small-group interactions
- Class discussions and reviews
- Short one-on-one sessions with the instructor
- Graded quizzes and tests
- The Limited Answer Key in the back of the book
- The online exercises available at **www.townsendpress.com**

In addition, since instructors using *Ten Steps to Building College Reading Skills* as a class text are permitted to reproduce any or all parts of this manual, you can selectively hand out copies of answers included here.

All of the exercises in the book are designed to make it easy to give clear and specific feedback. If students are going to learn to read and think more effectively, then they need clear, logical, specific responses to their efforts. This book enables teachers to provide such feedback.

Outlining, Mapping, and Summarizing

To take thoughtful, effective study notes, students need to learn three essential techniques: outlining, mapping, and summarizing. All three techniques often require students to identify the main idea and the major supporting details of a selection. But while educators agree that these three techniques are important for students to learn, they are all too seldom taught.

The book gives students instruction and practice in all three techniques. Passages in the "Supporting Details" and the two "Relationships" chapters, as well as all of the reading selections in Part Two and the three additional readings in this manual, are followed by an outlining, a mapping, or a summarizing activity. To complete many of these activities, students must look closely at the basic organization of the selection. They must think carefully about what they have read by asking two key questions: "What is the point?" and "What is the support for that point?" As students apply the techniques from one selection to the next and get specific feedback on their efforts, they will develop their ability to think in a clear and logical way.

Readability Levels . . . and Their Limitations

Below are the readability grade levels for the text of the book itself and the twenty reading selections. Because the book has been prepared on a computer, and there are now software programs that determine readability, it has been possible to do a complete readability evaluation for each reading, rather than merely sampling excerpts from the materials.

Please remember, however, that there are limits to the reliability and validity of readability scores. For instance, a readability formula cannot account for such significant factors as student interest, prior knowledge of a subject, the number of examples provided to explain concepts, and the overall clarity and logic of the writing.

Thus, while "Responsibility" has a readability level of 6th grade, it is a sophisticated adult piece that may be more challenging to students than, for example, "Disaster and Friendship," which has a reading level of 8. And while "Dealing with Feelings" has a readability level of 10, its extremely clear organization makes it a piece that developmental students can understand. I respect readability levels, but I also take them with a grain of salt, and I have kept other factors in mind while determining the sequence of readings.

Material	***Word Count***	***Reading Level***
Text of *Ten Steps*		8
Part One		
1. Responsibility	724	6
2. All the Good Things	1161	5
3. Group Pressure	937	7
4. A Door Swings Open	1401	7
5. Body Language	1335	9
6. Behind Closed Doors: Violence in the Family	1206	9
7. Wired for Touch	1622	7
8. A Path to Marriage	2306	6
9. Lighting a Match	1148	7
10. Do It Better!	2982	6

Material	*Word Count*	*Reading Level*
Part Two		
1. Winners, Losers, or Just Kids?	743	9
2. Owen, the Stray Cat	1409	6
3. Eye Contact	891	9
4. Disaster and Friendship	1661	8
5. Read All About It	1443	6
6. Adult Children at Home	1383	8
7. How to Make It in College, Now That You're Here	2640	7
8. False Ideas About Reading	1250	8
9. Dealing with Feelings	1661	10
10. Childhood Stress and Resilience	1339	10

A Final Note

Writing a book that contains hundreds of explanations and activities is a bit like being in a ball game where one steps up to the batter's box an almost countless number of times. One tries to get as many hits and extra-base hits as possible: to explain every concept so that students really understand it; to provide readings and practices that both interest students and teach the skills. One tries not to hit any foul balls. Hopefully there are not too many in this Fifth Edition of a book that has benefited from a great deal of teacher and student feedback.

Realistically, though, you might find that despite my best efforts, some items may not work. If they don't, and/or if you or your students are confused or uncertain about certain items, let me know so that I can consider making changes in the next printing or revision of the book. Send a note to me at Townsend Press, 439 Kelley Drive, West Berlin, NJ 08091. Alternatively, call Townsend Press at its toll-free number: 1-800-772-6410; send a fax to 1-800-225-8894; or send e-mail to **cs@townsendpress.com**; your comments will be passed on to me. And if you have a question, a Townsend editor will get back to you with an answer very shortly.

My thanks in advance for your help in my effort to keep improving the book!

John Langan

A PROFESSIONAL CONTRACT

FOR FIFTEEN WEEKS TOGETHER

between

____

(Student's name here)

and

____

(Instructor's name here)

Welcome to *(name of course)* ____________________________________. Counting today, we will be spending fifteen weeks together. How successful we are will depend on how well we follow a business contract that I would like you to read and sign, and that I will then sign and return to you. Here are the terms of the contract.

MY ROLE IN THE CONTRACT

My role will be to help you practice and master important reading and writing and thinking and learning skills. I will try to present these communication skills clearly and to give you interesting and worthwhile practice materials. I will conduct this as a skills course—not a lecture course where you could borrow a friend's notes afterwards. Typically several skills will be explained briefly in class, and you will then spend most of the class time practicing those skills, making them your own. You will be learning in the best possible way: through doing.

Why learn these skills?

I promise you that the skills will be of real value to you in all the other courses you take in college. They will make you a better reader, writer, thinker, and learner, and they can dramatically increase your chance for success in school.

The skills can be just as valuable for the career work you are likely to do in the future. Consider that America is no longer an industrial society where many people work on farms or in factories. Instead, most jobs now involve providing services or processing information. More than ever, communication skills are the tools of our trade. This course will be concerned directly with helping you learn and strengthen the communication skills that will be vital for job success in the 21st century.

YOUR ROLE IN THE CONTRACT

Experiencing the course

Your role in this contract will be to come to every class and to give a full effort. Much of the value and meaning of this skills course will come from what happens in class, so you must be here on a steady basis. Imagine trying to learn another skill without being present: for example, imagine learning how to drive without the *experience* of actually being in the car and working with the controls and getting feedback from your instructor. How much would you learn about the skill of driving if you relied only on the notes of a classmate? In a similar way, to really learn communication skills, you need direct experience and practice. So if you miss classes, you are in effect missing the course.

Shaping your attitude

Some people start college with a "high-school mindset." They are passive; they do the minimum they need to get by; their attention is elsewhere; they are like the living dead—and the American high-school system (and watching thousands of hours of television) may be to blame. Gradually these people realize that college is not high school: they don't have to be in college, and they are no longer part of the sad game played out in many high schools, where they receive a free ride and promotion no matter how little they do.

If your attitude about learning has been hurt by what happened in high school, then part of your role is to change your attitude. You can do so, and this contract will help.

Understanding sick days and personal days

You should try not to miss *any* classes. But in the professional environment of this class, like in the work world, everyone is entitled to a set number of sick days as well as "personal days"—unexplained absences. In this course, you will have a total of *(insert number)* _____ such days—which can cover such real-world happenings as sickness, car breakdowns, or even the death of someone you know. If you missed more than this amount of time in a real-world job contract, you would be let go. (Only in some extraordinary situation, such as an extended illness confirmed by a doctor's report, might an exception apply.) The professional terms of the work world will apply here: if you miss more than _____ classes, you cannot pass the course.

YOUR ROLE IF YOU MISS CLASS

If you do miss a class, you are responsible for getting the homework for the following week's class. To do so, call a classmate. Write down the names and phone numbers of two people in the room. (For now, use the people sitting on either side of you; you can always change these names later.)

Classmate # 1: *Name* ______________________________ *Phone* __________________

Classmate # 2: *Name* ______________________________ *Phone* __________________

Note that you **must** turn in all homework assignments or you **cannot pass the course**.

If a test or tests are given on a day you miss class, you cannot ordinarily make up these tests. Instead, you will receive a grade of M (Missing) for each missed test. When all your grades are averaged at the end of the semester, three M's will be omitted; the rest will convert to zeros.

YOUR COMMITMENT

I've read this contract, and the terms seem fair to me. (I like the fact that this college class is being treated as a professional situation, and I'm learning the ground rules up front.) I accept the responsibility and the challenge to make this course worth my time and money.

____ ________________________

Signed by (your name here) *Date*

____

Witnessed by the instructor

OR: If you don't want to sign this, please meet with me after this class to talk about why.

ANSWERS TO THE TESTS IN THE BOOK

Answers to the Review and Mastery Tests in Part One

DICTIONARY USE:
Review Test 1

1. B
2. C
3. A
4. A
5. E

DICTIONARY USE:
Review Test 2

A. 1. O
2. B
3. F
4. F
5. O

B. 6. cabinet
7. circus
8. design
9. gingerbread
10. dynamite

C. 11. determination
12. savor
13. humanize
14. profile
15. lunatic
16. humanize
17. Second
18. First
19. Fourth
20. Five

DICTIONARY USE:
Mastery Test 1

A. 1. B
2. B
3. B
4. 2
5. 1
6. B
7. 2
8. A
9. 1
10. 2

B. 11. tuna
12. freeze
13. tendency
14. parallel
15. accelerate

C. 16. im•pair ĭm-pâr′
17. sa•dis•tic sə-dĭs′tĭk
18. in•ev•i•ta•ble ĭn-ĕv′ĭ-tə-bəl
19. ap•pre•hen•sive ăp′rĭ-hĕn′sĭv
20. ster•e•o•type stĕr′ē-ə-tīp′

DICTIONARY USE:
Mastery Test 4

A. 1. B
2. B
3. A
4. 2
5. 1
6. B
7. A
8. A
9. 1
10. 2

B. 11. verb, noun
12. verb, noun, adjective
13. verb, noun, adjective
14. verb, adjective
15. noun, verb

C. 16. strategies
17. alumni
18. mothers-in-law
19. crises
20. passers-by (*or* passersby)

DICTIONARY USE:
Review Test 3

A. 1. scape•goat skāp′gōt′
2. ex•haust ĭg-zôst′
3. de•ci•sion dĭ-sĭzh′ən
4. cel•e•brate sĕl′ə-brāt′
5. re•cip•ro•cate rĭ-sĭp′rə-kāt′

B. 6. preposition, adverb
7. noun, verb
8. memories
9. livelier, liveliest
10. To drench thoroughly or cover with or as if with a liquid

DICTIONARY USE:
Mastery Test 2

A. 1. A
2. 3
3. A
4. B
5. C
6. A
7. 3
8. C
9. B
10. B

B. 11. concede
12. retrieve
13. pessimist
14. illuminate
15. inevitable

C. 16. as•pire ə-spīr′
17. rep•ri•mand rĕp′rə-mănd′
18. prin•ci•pal prĭn′sə-pəl
19. ter•mi•nate tûr′mə-nāt′
20. i•mag•i•na•tion ĭ-măj′ə-nā′shən

DICTIONARY USE:
Mastery Test 5
(Wording of definitions may vary.)

1. ăn′ĭk-dōt; an entertaining short story about an event
2. kŏm′pər-ə-bəl; similar; able to be compared
3. skĕp′tĭ-kəl; doubting, questioning
4. ĭm-pōz′ĭs; takes unfair advantage
5. dĭ-lēt′; to cross out or erase; remove
6. ĭg-zŏt′ĭk; foreign; from a different part of the world; strange or different in an appealing way
7. sə-sĕp′tə-bəl; likely to be affected (with)
8. plô′zə-bəl; seemingly or apparently valid, likely, or acceptable
9. străt′ə-jē; a plan of action intended to accomplish a specific goal
10. fō′bē-ə; a continuing, abnormal extreme fear of a particular thing or situation

DICTIONARY USE:
Review Test 4

Vocabulary

1. ə-mē′nə-bəl *or* ə-mĕn′ə-bəl
2. Second
3. Adjective
4. lo͞o′dĭ-krəs
5. First
6. Verb
7. re•spon•si•bil•i•ty (6 syllables)
8. id•i•ot•i•cal•ly (6 syllables)
9. A
10. A

Reading

1. B
2. D
3. C
4. D
5. D
6. C
7. B
8. A
9. B
10. B

DICTIONARY USE:
Mastery Test 3

A. 1. B
2. 3
3. A
4. B
5. A
6. C
7. 3
8. A
9. C
10. C

B. 11. exercise
12. deceive
13. finally
14. gullible
15. persistent

C. 16. e•lapse ĭ-lăps′
17. du•bi•ous do͞o′bē-əs
18. an•ti•dote ăn′tĭ-dōt′
19. in•gen•ious ĭn-jēn′yəs
20. per•se•ver•ance pûr′sə-vîr′əns

DICTIONARY USE:
Mastery Test 6
(Wording of definitions may vary.)

1. ĭ-lĕj′ə-bəl; not able to be read or deciphered
2. dĭ-spûrs′; to move in different directions; scatter
3. yo͞o-năn′ə-məs; based on or characterized by complete agreement
4. prə-pĕld′; caused to move forward
5. lē′thəl; able to cause death; deadly
6. prŏp′ə-găn′də; ideas spread to support or oppose a cause
7. sŭt′l; hardly noticeable; not obvious
8. ĭ-lo͞o′mə-nāt′; to provide or brighten with light
9. ôl′tərd; changed or made different; modified
10. ə-rĭj′ə-nāt′ĭd; came into being; started

VOCABULARY IN CONTEXT: Review Test 1

1. C
2. A
3. B
4. C
5. A

VOCABULARY IN CONTEXT: Review Test 2

A. 1. B

B. 2. C
3. C
4. D
5. B

C. 6. D violations
7. E warning
8. B lazy
9. C messy
10. A clear and brief

VOCABULARY IN CONTEXT: Review Test 3

A. 1. C
2. C

B. 3. H small
4. G reward
5. B encourage
6. C expensive

C. 7. C catch and eat
8. A attracts
9. D closes
10. E danger

VOCABULARY IN CONTEXT: Review Test 4

1. B
2. D
3. A
4. B
5. C
6. A
7. B
8. C
9. A
10. B

VOCABULARY IN CONTEXT: Mastery Test 1

A. 1. C
2. B

B. 3. Examples: *she missed two weeks of classes because of a strep throat, had all her books stolen just before finals;* A
4. Examples: *firing teachers, doing away with sports;* D

C. 5. show off
6. signal

D. 7. Antonym, *dirty*; D
8. Antonym, *interest*; D

E. 9. A
10. D

VOCABULARY IN CONTEXT: Mastery Test 2

A. 1. A

B. 2. Examples: *ignoring his memos, making fun of him behind his back;* D
3. Examples: *brown spots, soft places, small holes in the skin;* A

C. 4. make clear
5. never happened before
6. die down

D. 7. Antonym, *cheerful*; A
8. Antonym, *forward*; D

E. 9. C
10. D

VOCABULARY IN CONTEXT: Mastery Test 3

1. A
2. C
3. D
4. B
5. C
6. B
7. C
8. A
9. C
10. D

VOCABULARY IN CONTEXT: Mastery Test 4

1. B
2. D
3. A
4. B
5. D
6. B
7. C
8. D
9. C
10. D

VOCABULARY IN CONTEXT: Mastery Test 5

A. 1. D
2. B
3. A
4. C
5. D

B. 6. A coating
7. H step forth
8. D enormous
9. F lie down
10. B drops off

VOCABULARY IN CONTEXT: Mastery Test 6

A. 1. A
2. C
3. B
4. B
5. A

B. 6. E get involved
7. A dangerous
8. B discouragement
9. D force
10. H stand up to

MAIN IDEAS:
Review Test 1

1. main idea
2. specific
3. topic
4. supported
5. detail

MAIN IDEAS:
Review Test 2

A. 1. position
2. utility
3. housing
4. sense
5. drug
6. ingredient
7. decoration
8. debt

B. *Answers will vary. Here are some possibilities:*
9–10. cat, dog
11–12. knife, needle
13–14. sandals, shoes
15–16. toast, coffee

C. A. S
B. S
C. P
D. S

MAIN IDEAS:
Review Test 3

A.

Group 1	Group 2	Group 3
A. MI	A. T	A. T
B. SD	B. SD	B. SD
C. SD	C. MI	C. MI
D. T	D. SD	D. SD

B. 13. B
14. 1
15. B
16. 4

C. 17. C
18. C

D. 19. A
20. B

MAIN IDEAS:
Review Test 4

1. B
2. C
3. A
4. B
5. D
6. C
7. C
8. D
9. A
10. A

MAIN IDEAS:
Mastery Test 1

A. 1. tree
2. metal
3. insect
4. sport

B. *Answers will vary. Possibilities:*
5–6. banana, grape
7–8. Mexico, Egypt
9–10. Thanksgiving, Christmas
11–12. murderer, robber

C.

Group 1	Group 2
A. S	A. S
B. S	B. S
C. P	C. S
D. S	D. P

MAIN IDEAS:
Mastery Test 2

A. 1. flower
2. furniture
3. illness
4. clothes

B. *Answers will vary. Possibilities:*
5–6. coffee, tea
7–8. canary, pigeon
9–10. flood, forest fire
11–12. getting married, graduation

C.

Group 1	Group 2
A. S	A. S
B. S	B. S
C. P	C. S
D. S	D. P

MAIN IDEAS:
Mastery Test 3

A.

Group 1	Group 2	Group 3
A. S	A. P	A. S
B. S	B. S	B. S
C. P	C. S	C. S
D. S	D. S	D. P

B.

Group 1	Group 2
A. SD	A. SD
B. T	B. SD
C. SD	C. MI
D. MI	D. T

MAIN IDEAS:
Mastery Test 4

A.

Group 1	Group 2	Group 3
A. P	A. S	A. S
B. S	B. S	B. P
C. S	C. S	C. S
D. S	D. P	D. S

B.

Group 1	Group 2
A. SD	A. MI
B. SD	B. SD
C. MI	C. T
D. T	D. SD

MAIN IDEAS:
Mastery Test 5

A. (1–4.)
A. S
B. S
C. P
D. S

B.

Group 1	Group 2
A. SD	A. SD
B. SD	B. MI
C. T	C. SD
D. MI	D. T

C. 13. A
14. C
15. C
16. C

D. 17. B
18. C
19. A
20. C

MAIN IDEAS:
Mastery Test 6

A. (1–4.)
A. S
B. S
C. P
D. S

B.

Group 1	Group 2
A. SD	A. T
B. MI	B. SD
C. T	C. SD
D. SD	D. MI

C. 13. C
14. B
15. C
16. C

D. 17. B
18. A
19. C
20. B

SUPPORTING DETAILS:
Review Test 1

1. details
2. main idea (*or* point)
3. map
4. B
5. A

SUPPORTING DETAILS:
Review Test 2

A.
Main idea: *People lie for five main reasons.*

1. To prevent discomfort
2. To avoid conflict
3. To be socially acceptable
4. To increase or decrease interaction with someone
5. To have greater control over a situation

B.
6. five main reasons
7. Another
8. also
9. In addition
10. Finally

SUPPORTING DETAILS:
Review Test 3

A. Main idea: *Colonial Americans experienced a number of dangerous medical treatments.*

- Bloodletting
- Sweating
- Purging
  - Forcing patients to swallow syrup that would make them vomit

B. 5. a number of dangerous medical treatments

Note: Wording of answers to the outlines and maps in these tests may vary.

SUPPORTING DETAILS:
Review Test 4

1. B
2. A
3. B
4. D
5. A
6. D
7. C
8. D
9. C
10. B

SUPPORTING DETAILS:
Mastery Test 1

A.
1. Write often.
2. Organize your material with an outline.
3. Write in a plain style.
4. Tighten your writing.
5. First of all
6. Also

B.
Main idea: *Here are candidates for the lowest circles of Hell.*

- Child molesters
- Selfish politicians
- Terrorists

10. Next, Last

SUPPORTING DETAILS:
Mastery Test 2

A.
1. Drug abuser cannot stop using or drinking.
2. Drug abuser turns into a different person when using.
3. User makes excuses for using drugs.
4. User will try to cover up drug use or will pretend it isn't that bad.
5. User will forget what happens while he or she is high or drunk.
6. Abuser will be the last to recognize he or she has a problem.

B.
Main idea: *Several theories explain why people yawn.*

- Boosts oxygen level in blood
- Helps body change its level of alertness
- Gives the body exercise

10. *Any two of the following:* One, second, another

SUPPORTING DETAILS:
Mastery Test 3

A.
1. Don't trust appearances.
   a. A dog wagging its tail isn't always friendly.
2. Be cautious.
   a. Let a dog see and sniff you before petting it.
3. Watch for warning signs.
   a. Dogs that stare with lowered heads are probably not friendly.

B.
Main idea: *Here are steps for effective written complaints.*

- Address complaint to person in charge.
- Write complaint in a clear, matter-of-fact way.
- Explain exactly what action you want taken.

10. First, Next, Finally

SUPPORTING DETAILS: Mastery Test 4

A. 1. Uniforms would save money for parents and children.
   b. They wouldn't have to buy designer jeans, fancy sneakers, and other high-priced clothing.
2. Students would not have to spend time worrying about clothes.
   b. They could concentrate on schoolwork and learning, not on making a fashion statement.
3. Uniforms would help all students get along better.
   b. Students from modest backgrounds would not have to feel inferior because of lower-cost clothes.

B.
Main idea: *A number of factors influence the pace of aging.*

- Genes
- Lifestyle
- Social forces
  - Older people who are lonely often age faster than those who are involved with others.

SUPPORTING DETAILS: Mastery Test 5

A. 1. Temperature
   a. If a workspace is too warm, workers become cranky and uncomfortable.
2. Color
   b. Blue soothes workers.
3. Lighting
   a. Bright, direct light encourages good listening, close concentration, and comfortable reading.

B.
Main idea: *Certain strategies can help heal family feuds.*

- Get people to share the blame
- Increase communication
  - Write notes, make phone calls, attend family events.
- Set realistic goals

SUPPORTING DETAILS: Mastery Test 6

A. 1. Through the eyes
   a. By glaring, people can show they are angry without saying a word.
2. Through facial expressions
   b. By looking at a face, one can tell if a person is sad, happy, afraid, or surprised.
3. Through body posture
   a. A person who is sitting upright or leaning forward shows great interest and attention.

B.
Main idea: *Mysteries are questions in life without satisfying answers.*

- Why is there so much hatred on the planet?
- How can good and evil exist together in the same person?
  - An admired person can turn out to be an abuser.
- Why do some wealthy Christians do little to help the poor?

> ***Note:*** *Wording of answers to the outlines and maps in these tests may vary.*

LOCATIONS OF MAIN IDEAS: Review Test 1

1. first
2. main idea
3. end
4. List
5. details

LOCATIONS OF MAIN IDEAS: Review Test 2

1. Sentence 1
2. Sentence 5
3. Sentence 2
4. Sentence 1

LOCATIONS OF MAIN IDEAS: Review Test 3

1. Sentence 2
2. Sentence 1
3. Sentence 1
4. Sentence 9

LOCATIONS OF MAIN IDEAS: Review Test 4

1. B
2. B
3. D
4. D
5. A
6. A
7. D
8. B
9. A
10. D

LOCATIONS OF MAIN IDEAS: Mastery Test 1

1. Sentence 5
2. Sentence 2
3. Sentence 1
4. Sentence 2
5. Sentence 1

LOCATIONS OF MAIN IDEAS: Mastery Test 2

1. Sentence 1
2. Sentence 2
3. Sentence 6
4. Sentence 3
5. Sentence 1

LOCATIONS OF MAIN IDEAS: Mastery Test 3

1. Sentence 2
2. Sentence 10
3. Sentence 2
4. Sentence 1
5. Sentence 1

LOCATIONS OF MAIN IDEAS: Mastery Test 4

1. Sentence 2
2. Sentence 5
3. Sentence 5
4. Sentence 2
5. Sentence 1

LOCATIONS OF MAIN IDEAS: Mastery Test 5

1. Sentence 6
2. Sentence 3
3. Sentence 3
4. Sentence 1
5. Sentence 9

LOCATIONS OF MAIN IDEAS: Mastery Test 6

1. Sentence 2
2. Sentence 1
3. Sentence 7
4. Sentence 3
5. Sentence 2

RELATIONSHIPS I:
Review Test 1

1. Transitions
2. organization
3. addition
4. time
5. main idea

RELATIONSHIPS I:
Review Test 2

A. 1. A
2. B

B. 3. C Before
4. B Another
5. D Then
6. A also

C. 7. First
8. Then
9. While
10. B

RELATIONSHIPS I:
Review Test 3

A. 1. First of all
2. Second
3. Then
4. Finally
5. When

B. 6. B
7. A
8. B
9. B
10. A

RELATIONSHIPS I:
Review Test 4

1. D
2. B
3. B
4. A
5. C
6. F
7. B
8. also
9. A
10. C

RELATIONSHIPS I:
Mastery Test 1

A. 1. A After
2. E then
3. D second
4. B Another
5. C Before

B. 6. When
7. After
8. then
9. Before
10. B

RELATIONSHIPS I:
Mastery Test 2

A. 1. A also
2. E second
3. D During
4. C before
5. B Another

B. 6. First of all
7. Secondly
8. Moreover
9. Finally
10. A

RELATIONSHIPS I:
Mastery Test 3

A. 1–4. 3, 4, 2, 1
5. A

B. 6. B

C. 7. When
8. After
9. then
10. B

RELATIONSHIPS I:
Mastery Test 4

A. 1–4. 4, 1, 3, 2
5. B

B. 6. A

C. 7. later
8. When
9. then
10. Now

RELATIONSHIPS I:
Mastery Test 5

A. 1. A
2–3. *Any two of the following:* First of all, second, Last

B. 4. B
5–6. *Any two of the following:* In 1814, when, Then, In a short time, While, Three years later

C. 7. A
8. One
9. Another
10. third

RELATIONSHIPS I:
Mastery Test 6

A. 1. B
2–3. *Any two of the following:* earliest, in 540 B.C., then, until 1456, After, By the 1800s, in 1852, next, in the 1980s, Today

B. 4. A
5–6. *Any two of the following:* First of all, Second, Also, final

C. 7. A
8–10.

Main idea: *For several reasons, some people find it hard to give appreciation or praise.*

Received little praise or appreciation themselves | Insecurity | Fear

RELATIONSHIPS II:
Review Test 1

1. C
2. B
3. C
4. A
5. C

RELATIONSHIPS II:
Review Test 2

A. 1. C
2. B

B. 3. C like
4. D Therefore
5. A For example
6. B however

C. 7. C
8. B
9. A
10. C

RELATIONSHIPS II:
Review Test 3

A. 1. C
2. differently *or* In contrast

B. 3. B
4. leading to *or* caused *or* As a result *or* led to

C. 5. A
6. example

D. 7. B
8. On the other hand *or* while *or* as opposed to

E. 9. C
10. effects *or* cause *or* effect

RELATIONSHIPS II:
Review Test 4

1. A
2. D
3. C
4. B
5. B
6. F
7. D
8. A
9. A
10. B

RELATIONSHIPS II:
Mastery Test 1

A. 1. C For example
2. A As a result
3. E just as
4. D however
5. B Because

B. 6. B
7. C
8. A
9. C
10. B

RELATIONSHIPS II:
Mastery Test 2

A. 1. A explanation
2. B For instance
3. E Therefore
4. C However
5. D same

B. 6. B
7. C
8. B
9. C
10. A

RELATIONSHIPS II:
Mastery Test 3

A. 1–4. 3, 2, 1, 4
5. C

B. 6. A
7. For instance

C. 8. B
9–10. *Any two of the following:* result, reasons, cause, reason, As a result, caused, Therefore

RELATIONSHIPS II:
Mastery Test 4

A. 1–4. 2, 3, 1, 4
5. D

B. 6. B
7. effects *or* As a result *or* effect *or* led to

C. 8. C
9. In contrast *or* while *or* However
10. In contrast *or* while *or* However

RELATIONSHIPS II:
Mastery Test 5

A. 1–4. 4, 3, 1, 2
5. D

B. 6. B
7. led to *or* affected by *or* result

C. 8. C
9–10. *Any two of the following:* difference, On the other hand, In contrast, But

RELATIONSHIPS II:
Mastery Test 6

A. 1. B
2–5. 1. Managers who lack enough knowledge or experience
2. Neglect
3. Poor record-keeping
4. Lack of money

B. 6. D
7–10.

Cold	*Flu*
2. Headaches may or may not occur.	1. Fever is typical.
	2. Headaches are likely.
	4. Victims may suffer extreme fatigue.

RELATIONSHIPS I and II:
Mastery Test 1

A. 1. A Because
2. C In addition
3. B For example
4. E On the other hand
5. D just like

B. 6. E Then
7. D such as
8. B Before
9. C However
10. A Another

RELATIONSHIPS I and II:
Mastery Test 2

A. 1. C
2. During *or* When *or* later *or* after *or* then *or* in 1955 *or* ten years after the war ended

B. 3. B
4. reasons *or* reason *or* cause

C. 5. A
6. effects *or* led to

D. 7. A
8. First *or* Another *or* third

E. 9. B
10. like *or* Similarly *or* Just as *or* alike

INFERENCES: Review Test 1

1. inferences
2. context
3. stated
4. useful
5. useful

INFERENCES: Review Test 2

A. 2, 4

B. 3. B
4. A
5. B

INFERENCES: Review Test 3

A. 1

B. 3, 5

C 3, 4

INFERENCES: Review Test 4

1. C
2. D
3. C
4. A
5. C
6. B
7. A
8. C
9. B
10. A

INFERENCES: Mastery Test 1

A. 1, 4, 5, 7

B. 5–6. B, C
7–8. B, C
9–10. A, D

INFERENCES: Mastery Test 2

A. 2, 3, 6, 8

B. 5–6. B, D
7–8. A, D
9–10. B, C

INFERENCES: Mastery Test 3

A. 1–2. B, D
3–4. B, D

B. 5–7. A, C, E
8–10. B, C, D

INFERENCES: Mastery Test 4

A. 1–2. A, C
3–4. A, D

B. 5–7. B, C, E
8–10. B, C, E

INFERENCES: Mastery Test 5

A. 1. C
2. A
3. C

B. 1, 3, 6, 7, 8

INFERENCES: Mastery Test 6

A. 1, 4, 6, 7

B. 3, 4, 5, 8

IMPLIED MAIN IDEAS: Review Test 1

1. implied
2. supporting details
3. narrow
4. broad
5. is bad (*or* is not worth seeing)

IMPLIED MAIN IDEAS: Review Test 2

A. 1. Come to a complete stop at the stop sign, or you'll get a ticket. *(Wording of answer may vary.)*

B. 2. A
3. B

C. 4. Books (*or* Novels *or* Movies)
5. Definitions

IMPLIED MAIN IDEAS: Review Test 3

A. 1. (Group 1) D
2. (Group 2) C
3. (Group 3) B

B. 4. D
5. B

IMPLIED MAIN IDEAS: Review Test 4

1. D
2. C
3. A
4. B
5. A
6. C
7. C
8. C
9. B
10. B

IMPLIED MAIN IDEAS: Mastery Test 1

A. 1. C

B. 2. B
3. B
4. C
5. A
6. B
7. C
8. C
9. B
10. A

IMPLIED MAIN IDEAS: Mastery Test 2

1. Tools
2. Sports (*or* Team sports *or* Professional sports)
3. Cookies
4. Workers
5. Crimes
6. Music (*or* Types of music)
7. Breakfast foods
8. Good working conditions
9. Wedding preparations
10. Ways to fail a course

(Wording of answers may vary.)

IMPLIED MAIN IDEAS: Mastery Test 3

1. C
2. B
3. C
4. A

IMPLIED MAIN IDEAS: Mastery Test 4

1. A
2. D
3. B
4. B

IMPLIED MAIN IDEAS: Mastery Test 5

1. C
2. A
3. B
4. C

IMPLIED MAIN IDEAS: Mastery Test 6

1. A
2. D
3. B
4. C

THE BASICS OF ARGUMENT: Review Test 1

1. general idea
2. support

3–5. point
support
support

THE BASICS OF ARGUMENT: Review Test 2

A. 1. D

B.

Group 1	Group 2
A. P	A. S
B. S	B. S
C. S	C. P
D. S	D. S

C. 10. A

THE BASICS OF ARGUMENT: Review Test 3

A. A. S
B. S
C. P
D. S

B. 5–7. A, D, E
8–10. A, C, E

THE BASICS OF ARGUMENT: Review Test 4

1. D	6. D
2. B	7. D
3. A	8. B
4. D	9. D
5. D	10. C

THE BASICS OF ARGUMENT: Mastery Test 1

A.

Group 1	Group 2
A. S	A. S
B. S	B. S
C. S	C. S
D. P	D. P

B. 9. B

C. 10. A

THE BASICS OF ARGUMENT: Mastery Test 2

A. 1–3. B, C, D
4–6. B, C, E
7–9. B, C, D

B. 10. C

THE BASICS OF ARGUMENT: Mastery Test 3

A.

Group 1	Group 2
A. S	A. P
B. S	B. S
C. P	C. S
D. S	D. S

B. 9. C

C. 10. B

THE BASICS OF ARGUMENT: Mastery Test 4

A. 1–3. A, B, D
4–6. A, B, D
7–9. A, C, D

B. 10. C

THE BASICS OF ARGUMENT: Mastery Test 5

A. A. P
B. S
C. S
D. S

B. 5–7. A, B, C

C. 8. B
9. A
10. B

THE BASICS OF ARGUMENT: Mastery Test 6

A. A. S
B. P
C. S
D. S

B. 5–7. B, C, E

C. 8. (Group 1) B
9. (Group 2) B
10. (Group 3) C

Answers to the Reading Selections in Part Two

1 WINNERS, LOSERS, OR JUST KIDS?

Vocabulary Questions		Comprehension Questions	
1. B	6. B flaunted	1. D	6. D
2. C	7. D morose	2. A	7. B
3. C	8. A endeared	3. B	8. D
4. D	9. E sheepish	4. C	9. A
5. A	10. C metamorphosis	5. B	10. C

Summarizing

1. C
2. C
3. A

2 OWEN, THE STRAY CAT

Vocabulary Questions		Comprehension Questions	
1. D	6. C sarcastically	1. D	6. D
2. B	7. E vigorously	2. C	7. D
3. D	8. B glints	3. C	8. C
4. A	9. A estimate	4. B	9. B
5. C	10. D twist	5. F	10. B

Outlining

3. When Carlin puts the kitten on the bathroom floor with food and water, the kitten is too weak to eat.
6. Three days later, Carlin takes the kitten to the vet for its first checkup.
7. A small boy at the vet's office names the stray kitten Owen.
8. When Owen disturbs Bob's sleep, Carlin and Bob argue over who is really responsible for the kitten being there.

3 EYE CONTACT

Vocabulary Questions		Comprehension Questions	
1. A	6. D torture	1. B	6. B
2. B	7. B obvious	2. D	7. C
3. B	8. C proposal	3. C	8. D
4. D	9. E various	4. C	9. C
5. C	10. A emphasis	5. D	10. A

Summarizing *(Note: Wording of answers may vary.)*

1. takes note of how effective they are at maintaining eye contact with their partners.
2. raise their hands to make additional comments until the speaker is finished.
3. tries to get his students to practice making eye contact with various adults in the school who aren't teachers.
4. look the cafeteria workers in the eye and say "May I" when asking for anything.
5. that the class is wonderful and that they appreciate the respect.

4 DISASTER AND FRIENDSHIP

Vocabulary Questions		Comprehension Questions	
1. B	6. E stereotyped	1. B	7. C
2. C	7. B intensified	2. A	8. A
3. C	8. C related	3. D	9. B
4. A	9. A bearing	4. B	10. D
5. C	10. D severely	5. C	
		6. *Any two of the following:* When, after, eventually	

Mapping

B—>*F*—>*E*—>D—>C—>A

5 READ ALL ABOUT IT

Vocabulary Questions		Comprehension Questions	
1. A	6. A chaos	1. B	6. B
2. D	7. D stunned	2. D	7. B
3. C	8. C landmark	3. A	8. C
4. B	9. E unique	4. C	9. T
5. B	10. B decipher	5. B	10. B

Summarizing *(Note: Wording of answers may vary.)*

1. distributing mail in a bank.
2. DeBlasio was offered a promotion.
3. a reading group
4. her friends about the problem she had with reading.

6 ADULT CHILDREN AT HOME

Vocabulary Questions		Comprehension Questions	
1. C	6. C phenomenon	1. C	6. D
2. B	7. B fixed	2. A	7. A
3. A	8. E ruefully	3. A	8. C
4. D	9. D precautions	4. D	9. C
5. A	10. A consent	5. F	10. T

Outlining

3. B
4. A
5. D
6. C

7 HOW TO MAKE IT IN COLLEGE

Vocabulary Questions		Comprehension Questions	
1. B	6. E relatively	1. B	6. A
2. A	7. C hurdle	2. C	7. B
3. A	8. A distracted	3. C	8. T
4. C	9. D maintain	4. C	9. D
5. B	10. B hermit	5. D	10. A

Outlining *(Note: Wording of answers may vary.)*

Central point: There are practical steps you can take to make yourself successful in college.

A2. Get into a study frame of mind.
A6. Review your textbook and your notes.
B2. Make up a study schedule.
B3. Use "to-do" lists.
C3. If your problems are overwhelming, see a counselor.

8 FALSE IDEAS ABOUT READING

Vocabulary Questions		Comprehension Questions	
1. B	6. B dry	1. B	6. C
2. C	7. C passive	2. D	7. B
3. A	8. E sound	3. B	8. D
4. B	9. D resources	4. B	9. D
5. D	10. A asserted	5. D	10. T

Outlining *(Note: Wording of answers may vary.)*

Central point: Three myths about reading keep people from becoming better readers.

1. The first myth is that every word must be read.
2. The second myth is that reading once is enough.
3. The third myth is that reading has to be work.

9 DEALING WITH FEELINGS

Vocabulary Questions		Comprehension Questions	
1. B	6. D perceived	1. B	7. For instance, example
2. D	7. E seethe	2. D	
3. C	8. A decipher	3. A	8. C
4. A	9. C inconsequential	4. A	9. B
5. B	10. B elated	5. C	10. C
		6. C	

Mapping *(Note: Wording of answers may vary.)*

Central point: There are three ways that people deal with their feelings: while each is appropriate at times, the last one is especially useful for educating others about how you want them to treat you.

Withholding feelings *means* keeping them inside.	Displaying feelings *means* expressing them through a nonverbal or verbal reaction.	Describing feelings *means* putting them into words.

10 CHILDHOOD STRESS AND RESILIENCE

Vocabulary Questions		Comprehension Questions	
1. B	6. A adverse	1. C	6. B
2. D	7. C console	2. A	7. D
3. C	8. B compensate	3. A	8. A
4. D	9. D resilience	4. B	9. D
5. C	10. E subject	5. C	10. B

Summarizing *(Note: Wording of answers may vary.)*

1. divorce or death of parents, hospitalization, poverty, wars, earthquake, homelessness, and violence
2. psychological
3. resilient children.
4. family, learning experiences, reduced risk, and compensating experiences.

Answers to the Combined-Skills Tests in Part Three

COMBINED SKILLS: Mastery Test 1

1. C
2. A
3. D
4. B
5. D
6. C
7. B
8. C

COMBINED SKILLS: Mastery Test 2

1. D
2. C
3. A
4. B
5. D
6. B
7. B
8. A

COMBINED SKILLS: Mastery Test 3

1. B
2. D
3. B
4. D
5. A
6. C
7. B
8. B

COMBINED SKILLS: Mastery Test 4

1. A
2. A
3. C
4. B
5. D
6. A
7. A
8. D

COMBINED SKILLS: Mastery Test 5

1. C
2. D
3. D
4. C
5. F
6. B
7. A
8. A

COMBINED SKILLS: Mastery Test 6

1. A
2. D
3. A
4. D
5. B
6. B
7. D
8. B

COMBINED SKILLS: Mastery Test 7

1. A
2. B
3. A
4. C
5. C
6. A
7. B
8. B

COMBINED SKILLS: Mastery Test 8

1. D
2. B
3. B
4. D
5. B
6. D
7. B
8. C

COMBINED SKILLS: Mastery Test 9

1. D
2. A
3. C
4. D
5. D
6. A
7. B
8. D

COMBINED SKILLS: Mastery Test 10

1. B
2. D
3. D
4. C
5. A
6. D
7. A
8. A

COMBINED SKILLS: Mastery Test 11

1. A
2. C
3. A
4. A
5. B
6. C
7. B
8. D

COMBINED SKILLS: Mastery Test 12

1. D
2. A
3. C
4. D
5. B
6. B
7. A
8. B

COMBINED SKILLS: Mastery Test 13

1. D
2. C
3. C
4. B
5. D
6. C
7. B
8. A

COMBINED SKILLS: Mastery Test 14

1. D
2. A
3. B
4. C
5. C
6. C
7. B
8. D

COMBINED SKILLS: Mastery Test 15

1. C
2. C
3. A
4. B
5. B
6. D
7. A
8. C

COMBINED SKILLS: Mastery Test 16

1. C
2. C
3. B
4. A
5. C
6. B
7. D
8. D

COMBINED SKILLS: Mastery Test 17

1. B
2. D
3. C
4. B
5. B
6. A
7. B
8. C

COMBINED SKILLS: Mastery Test 18

1. B
2. A
3. F
4. D
5. D
6. C
7. A
8. B

SUGGESTED ANSWERS TO THE DISCUSSION QUESTIONS IN PART ONE

Note: The numbers in parentheses refer to paragraphs in the reading. Also, for some questions, additional related questions have been included to enhance class discussion.

1 RESPONSIBILITY, M. Scott Peck

1. *Peck says that some people will go to ridiculous lengths to avoid assuming responsibility for their personal problems. What is ridiculous about the sergeant's behavior? About the young wife's behavior?*

   Both the sergeant and the young wife go to absurd lengths to justify their behavior. The sergeant invents numerous excuses for not pursuing activities other than drinking, even activities that he claims to enjoy. He then claims that it's the lack of pleasurable activities that drive him to drink. The young wife would rather complain and even attempt suicide (weakly) than make the small effort of learning to drive a stick shift.

   What might the sergeant and the young wife have done if they had assumed responsibility for their problems?

2. *What details might Peck have included in this selection if he had chosen students as examples? What responsibilities do students typically avoid? What excuses do they make?*

   Students frequently fail to take responsibility for their academic performance. Rather than do what is necessary to do well in class, they blame other people and circumstances for their own choices: "My best friend moved, and I had to help him," "I didn't study because I forgot to take my book home," "I didn't know there was a test," "I had to go to a party, so I didn't have time to write my paper."

3. *Peck writes that "we must accept responsibility for a problem before we can solve it." What does he mean by that? Do you agree? Use examples from your own life or someone else's to support your view.*

   Peck means that ultimately, the only person with power over an individual's problems is that individual. If we fool ourselves into believing that our problem is not our own responsibility, then we can allow ourselves to avoid taking responsibility. Only when we say, "This is my problem—not someone else's," can we begin to solve the problem. Students' opinions of Peck's statement will vary. Their personal examples will give them a chance to consider what taking personal responsibility for one's problems means.

4. *Why do you think it's so difficult for people to take responsibility for their problems?*

   Answers will vary. Reasons for people's reluctance to take responsibility include the following:

   - Laziness—it's just easier not to
   - Fear—a person may be afraid of taking responsibility and then failing or being in an new, unfamiliar situation
   - The lure of gaining sympathy from others by complaining about a situation, rather than trying to fix it.

2 ALL THE GOOD THINGS, Sister Helen P. Mrosla

1. *In this story, we read of two classroom incidents involving Sister Helen and her students. In one, she briefly taped a third-grader's mouth closed. In another, she encouraged junior-high students to think of things they liked about one another. In your opinion, what do these two incidents tell about Sister Helen? What kind of teacher was she? What kind of person?*

   Both classroom incidents reveal Sister Helen as a sincere, well-meaning teacher. In the first incident, she is inexperienced; by the time of the second incident, she has become a skilled teacher with excellent judgment. In telling about the first classroom incident, Sister Helen shows her objectivity and lack of pride by saying of herself, "I made a novice teacher's mistake" (3). Her action in taping Mark's mouth shut seems to embarrass her, but she feels she has to carry through on her promise. The second classroom incident involves a mature teacher who is able to judge her students' mood and instinctively react in a way that would accomplish her purpose, and more. Her decision to have the students write down nice things about one another demonstrates her desire to see her students enjoy school and appreciate one another, not merely learn their academic subjects.

2. *Why do you think so many of Sister Helen's students kept their lists for so long? Why were the lists so important to them? What souvenir of the past have you kept for a long time? What does it mean to you?*

   Students probably kept the lists because they represented something very positive. The lists were concrete evidence of qualities others liked about them, something they might otherwise have never, or rarely, encountered. The lists could be read again and again through the years. People rarely have a chance to experience praise in such a lasting, concrete form. Students' answers about souvenirs they treasure will reveal things that are important to them.

   Do you remember something positive that was said about you years ago? How important was that comment to your self-image?

3. *At the end of the story, Sister Helen tells us that she "cried for Mark and for all his friends who would never see him again." Do you think she might have been crying for other reasons, too? Explain what they might be.*

   Sister Helen might also have been moved by the realizations that her assignment had been so valued and that her students had been in such need of appreciation.

4. *"All the Good Things" has literally traveled around the world. Not only has it been reprinted in numerous publications, but many readers have sent it out over the Internet for others to read. Why do you think so many people love this story? Why do they want to share it with others?*

   The story reminds readers of how much we all want and need the affirmation of others. Some people who read it are probably moved to get in touch with loved ones and let them know that they are appreciated. The sharing of Sister Helen's story may be an indirect way of reminding others to tell friends and relatives, especially young people, their good points.

3 GROUP PRESSURE, Rodney Stark

1. *Were you at all surprised by the results of Solomon Asch's experiment? If you had been one of the subjects, do you think you would have stuck to your answers, or would you have gone along with the group? Why?*

   Students are likely to express surprise at the large number (75 percent) of subjects who eventually went along with the erroneous conclusions, at least some of the time. Some will probably insist they would never bow to group pressure and deny the evidence of their own eyes. Others may be sympathetic to the idea that it would be difficult to resist the temptation to fit in with the group by seeming to agree with the others' conclusions.

2. *What reasons might the subjects in the Asch experiment have had for eventually giving in and accepting the group's wrong answers?*

   Answers will vary. Some subjects might have begun to doubt their own judgment or thought they'd misunderstood the instructions. Others might have reacted to the feeling that they were being tricked or that they would mess up the experiment in some way if they insisted on giving an answer contrary to the others.

   What characteristic or characteristics do you think are responsible for "the behavior of those who steadfastly refused to accept the group's misjudgments" (9)?

3. *Stark refers to the Asch experiment as a "weak group situation," one in which the group is made up of strangers and the stakes are not very high. What might a "strong group situation" be? Give examples.*

   If a weak group situation includes strangers and relatively unimportant stakes, a strong group situation would involve acquaintances or even more closely-related people and more important consequences. An example of a strong group situation might be a boy whose family and friends strongly oppose his dating a girl of another race or religion. The group would be made up of people he's strongly influenced by, and the stakes (the possible loss of their support and friendship) would be high. Other examples: a gang pressuring a member to commit an illegal act, and a group of students expecting a friend to help them make fun of another student who is perceived as different.

4. *Have you ever been in a situation when you wanted to resist group pressure? What was the situation, and why did you want to resist? What could you have done to resist?*

   Answers will vary. Most people have faced situations where they felt torn between their individual desires and the desires of a group.

4 A DOOR SWINGS OPEN, Roxanne Black

1. *When Black enters the hospital, she becomes aware of an "alternate world" that "had existed all along, behind my formerly sunny, innocent life." What is this "alternate world"? What, in particular, does she find surprising about it?*

   The "alternate world" Black experiences when she enters the hospital is one in which children suffer as the result of serious illness and accidents. Prior to being hospitalized with lupus, Black, who had never known a sick child before, had thought of her life as "sunny" and "innocent" (31). Now that she is in a hospital filled with sick children, she realizes that life is not at all sunny for many children. What she finds particularly surprising is that this world "had existed all along" (31) without her being aware of it.

2. *Black quotes Graham Greene, who wrote, "There's always one moment in childhood when the door opens and lets the future in." What might this statement mean? According to Black's story, when did this experience happen to her? Why do you think she was so upset afterward?*

   Black writes that, for her, "The door had swung open, and I had been pushed through to the other side" after she learned that her hospital roommate Michelle had died during open-heart surgery (40–41). Since "the door opens" for Black after Michelle's death, Graham Greene's statement can be taken to mean that there is always a moment in childhood when we are faced with the adult realization that life isn't "fair" and that "the young and innocent could be lost" (41). Students should infer that Black was upset after Michelle's death because she had grown quite fond of the three-year-old, whom she described as being "energetic," "lively," and "vital" (26, 30). Furthermore, Michelle had given her a parting gift of a drawing before being taken to surgery. Perhaps Black also realizes that if Michelle can die at a young age, then so too might she. For the first time in her life, Black has experienced death—which waits in the future for all of us—first-hand.

3. *Have you ever known anyone who, like Black, suffers from chronic illness? If so, how does it affect his or her life? What adjustments has the person made in order to live with this condition?*

   Answers will vary. Adjustments to living with chronic illness may include taking medication on a schedule; self-testing (as with diabetes); maintaining a special diet; using wheelchairs, walkers, and other assistive devices; undergoing dialysis (in the case of kidney failure); frequent hospitalizations; and the assistance of caregivers.

4. *Do you remember a moment in your life when "the door opened and let the future in"? Describe the event, and explain what it made you realize.*

   Answers will vary. Students may mention the serious illness or death of a friend or family member as being the moment "the door opened and let the future in" for them. Or they might describe a happier event, such as being accepted by a college or the birth of a child.

5 BODY LANGUAGE, Beth Johnson

1. *How aware of body language were you before you read this article? After reading it, might you behave any differently in situations where you are meeting people for the first time? Explain.*

   Students will realize that they can get a sense of someone they meet not just through what the person says, but by his or her body language. Examples will vary.

   Students might enjoy choosing one environment in which to note body language for a few moments and then reporting on their observations the next day.

2. *What is some of the "vocabulary" of classroom body language? Consider both students' and teachers' nonverbal communication.*

   Some common classroom body language includes the teacher's expression of authority by standing over a sitting student, or his or her crouching down to a student's level when trying to establish a closer connection. An instructor may stop and stare hard at a misbehaving student to demand his or her attention. Students show they are bored, attentive, distracted, or annoyed by such nonverbal actions as slumping in their seats with their eyes closed, sitting up straight and making eye contact with the instructor, playing with a pencil, or rolling their eyes and shifting position.

3. *Johnson gives several examples of ritual and body language in courtship. What others could you add?*

   Answers will vary. In seeking answers to this question, students can think of recent social scenes and personal relationships.

4. *Johnson writes, "Body language can be explained only within its context. . . . you shouldn't expect to find a 'dictionary' for reliable definitions of . . . tapping toes." Give some examples in which certain body language has different meanings in different situations. For example, what* are *some different meanings that tapping toes might have?*

   The interpretation of body language depends very much on the context in which it occurs. For instance, tapping one's toes could mean that one was impatient, or nervous, or that one was keeping time with some real or imaginary music. Or one person touching another's hand during a conversation could be a gesture of sympathy or of romantic interest, or it could be a way of emphasizing a point.

6 BEHIND CLOSED DOORS: VIOLENCE IN THE FAMILY, Michael S. Bassis, Richard J. Gelles, and Ann Levine

1. *Why do you think the researchers "asked a representative sample of Americans how they resolved family conflicts" instead of using official statistics such as police reports? What did their method accomplish that relying on official statistics would not have accomplished?*

   Official statistics reflect only the small percentage of violent incidents that are actually reported to police. Asking a representative sample of families gives a much broader picture of the violence that is a daily occurrence in many homes.

2. *What myths about family violence did the survey disprove? Why might these myths have existed in the first place?*

   The author lists three myths that were disproved: that violence among family members is rare (3); that family violence is primarily a problem of the poor and uneducated (3–4); and that people who abuse a loved one are mentally ill (5). These myths may have arisen out of people's need to idealize the family home as a safe, loving place and to convince themselves that they could not fall victim to family violence—that it's something that happens to "other" people.

3. *Were you or was someone you know ever punished with physical force as a child? If so, what do you think have been the effects of this use of force?*

   Answers will vary.

4. *What can society—for instance, schools, religious institutions, government, the media—do to prevent further violence in families?*

   Answers will vary. The schools, media, churches, and other institutions could help by speaking out openly about how widespread family violence is. Many people involved in family violence decline to seek help because they think their family must be very unusual or abnormal, and they are embarrassed to admit the problem. Employers could offer counseling services as part of their employee benefit packages, so that workers who are under stress could deal with their problems, rather than take them out on their families.

7 WIRED FOR TOUCH, Deborah Grandinetti

1. *Why do you think Grandinetti begins the selection with the anecdote about the young man who had been badly burned? How does this anecdote relate to her central point?*

   Students should infer that Grandinetti begins with the anecdote about the badly burned young man in order to arouse the curiosity of readers, who immediately begin to wonder whether the young man will be able to adjust to the death of his mother and "be in the world without her" (10). The fact that the massage therapist helps the young man to accept himself convincingly illustrates Grandinetti's central point—that we are indeed "wired for touch." If she had begun the selection with some scientific facts about touch or with another, shorter anecdote, the selection would not have the emotional impact that it does.

2. *Grandinetti mentions people such as waitresses and financial advisors who make a point of gently touching their clients. How would you feel about being touched in such situations? Do you think it would make you more willing to give a higher tip or take a risk with your money? Or might you react in some other way? Explain.*

   Answers will vary. Some students may indicate that being touched by a waitress or financial advisor might indeed make them more likely to give a higher tip or take a financial risk since, as Grandinetti writes, a woman's touch evokes "the feelings of security that comes from a mother's touch" (18). Others may state that being touched by a stranger might make them feel as if they were being manipulated. As a result, they would not be more likely to part with more money.

   Would the touch of a waiter or male financial advisor have the same effect as that of a waitress or female financial advisor? Why or why not?

3. *Some families often express affection through touch, while others don't. What was (or is) true of your family? Do you think that their expression of affection through touch (or lack of it) has affected you? Explain.*

   Answers will vary. Those students who indicate that their family did express affection through touch might be more inclined to express affection that way than those students whose families did not use touch to express affection. On the other hand, some students may say that they make a conscious effort to express affection through touch because they realize that their family members did not do this, and that as a result, something important was missing from their lives.

4. *Most people would say that sight and hearing are the most important senses. However, Grandinetti feels differently. Do you agree with Grandinetti's conclusion that we are indeed "wired for touch"? Why or why not?*

   Although answers may vary, most students will probably agree that Grandinetti makes a strong case for the importance of touch. She presents several anecdotes that illustrate the positive impact touch can have on a person's psychological well-being. She also presents measurable effects of caring touch (16) and psychological studies that confirm the importance of touch (17, 18). In paragraphs 19 through 22, she presents evidence that supports the statement that touch is our "first language" and essential for healthy development.

8 A PATH TO MARRIAGE, Jean Sutton

1. *After reading what Jean Sutton has to say about relationships, do you think she believes in "love at first sight?" Why or why not?*

   Students should infer that Sutton does not believe in love at first sight for the following reasons:

   - She waited a full year after she had met her future husband Rod before beginning to date him.
   - During the period when they were "just friends," she was able to evaluate his attitude toward life, and came to appreciate him for his respect for women (11–13) and the elderly (17), as well as his strong work ethic (15). In fact, it is Rod's consideration for an elderly woman, not any immediate attraction, that "seals the deal" for Sutton in terms of marrying him (17).
   - Finally, she states, "A good rule of thumb is to know your mate through at least four seasons before you get married. Don't rush!" (22)

2. *Sutton says several times that it's more important to pay attention to what a romantic partner does than what he says. Do you think her advice is worthwhile? Why or why not?*

   Many students will probably agree with Sutton's belief that "words are easy" and that actions are a far more accurate indicator of how one will be treated by a potential romantic partner. They may support their opinion by providing examples of how they or someone they know was "sweet-talked" by someone whose actions did not support his or her words.

3. *Sutton mentions that her husband, Rod, was teased by some male friends for not having a child sooner. Why do you think men would put pressure on each other that way? What did you think of Rod's response?*

   One reason men put pressure on each other to father children may be that they are insecure about their own masculinity. Fathering a child is tangible proof that they are indeed "masculine." Additionally, they may feel "tied down" by having to provide for children and envious of men who do not have that responsibility. Students may point out that when men pressure Rod to father a child, they do not seem to be considering the well-being of the child—only their own "values."

   Students will probably agree that Rod acts wisely in not letting such criticism influence him since, as Sutton says, "bringing a new human being into the world is a very serious decision, and not something to be done lightly" (20).

4. *Jean Sutton describes her husband Rod as a true partner. Based on her description, what qualities must a mate have to be considered a true partner? Are those qualities ones that are important to you? Are there others you would add?*

   Based on her description of Rod, students may conclude that to be considered a true partner, a mate should have

   - values that are similar to those of one's spouse
   - good communication skills
   - enough self-confidence to not feel threatened by the spouse's career
   - respect for women and the elderly
   - the ability and desire to contribute financially to a marriage (a strong work ethic)
   - a willingness to share in child-rearing

   Students might also mention other qualities, such as

   - a good sense of humor
   - gentleness
   - faithfulness
   - sex appeal

9 LIGHTING A MATCH, Regina Ruiz

1. *During the years of her unhappy marriage, Ruiz told herself, "The children need you, and you cannot admit failure to your parents back in Venezuela." Do these seem to you like understandable reasons for remaining in an unhappy relationship? Are they* good *reasons?*

   Most people find such reasons understandable. But one could argue that they are not good reasons since they don't address the problem of a very unhappy relationship. Children raised in an unhappy marriage may take that as their model for future relationships, believing that it is normal to be unhappy. And most family members or friends would ultimately rather see a person happy and fulfilled than living in a miserable situation.

2. *Ruiz writes that after she enrolled in college, she was proud of herself "for not falling into the garbage pit waiting so close by." What do you think she means by the words "the garbage pit waiting so close by"? Have you ever made a choice that you feel either saved you from or dropped you into "a garbage pit?"*

   For Ruiz, "the garbage pit" probably meant a life of frustration and fear—i.e., the life she would have lived if she had not taken steps toward a better one. She could easily have been overwhelmed by her problems and gone through the rest of her life feeling she was a failure. Answers will vary concerning what students have seen as "the garbage pit" waiting for them—but they will reflect students' understanding of the results of bad decisions in challenging circumstances.

   Do you know someone, who like Ruiz, had to choose between accepting a bad situation or taking steps toward a better life? Tell about that person.

3. *Like Ruiz, adults who return to college often have a difficult time balancing the demands of their work, family, and classes. What challenges do you face as a student? What ways have you found to deal with them?*

   Answers will vary.

4. *Ruiz briefly explains her decision to become a nurse. Why have you chosen your own course of study? What about it interests you? What do you hope it will offer to you after college?*

   Answers will vary.

10 DO IT BETTER! Ben Carson, M.D., with Cecil Murphey

1. *Why did Bennie consider himself "the dumbest kid in class"? How did his image of himself affect his schoolwork?*

   Bennie Carson was a new student at his school and had gotten off to a poor start by giving frequent wrong answers in class. The other students had laughed at him and labeled him "dumb." Deciding that they were right, Carson made no effort to improve his grades and instead escaped into activities that he enjoyed: watching TV and playing outside.

2. *The author recalls his failure in the classroom as an eight-year-old child by writing, "Perhaps I wasn't emotionally able to learn much." Why does he make this statement? What things in a child's home or social life might interfere with his or her education?*

   Carson was distracted by his parents' marital troubles, their separation, and the disappearance of his father. Children whose lives outside of school are unsettled often find it hard to concentrate on schoolwork. Parents' problems, poverty, fighting, or substance abuse in the home are a few of the factors that could interfere with a child's readiness to learn.

3. *Part of Carson's mother's plan for helping her sons to improve their schoolwork was limiting their television watching to two programs a week. How much of a role do you think this limit played in the success of her plan? Do you agree with her that unrestricted television watching can be harmful to children?*

   It seems clear that restricting the boys' TV watching did benefit them. They used their former TV-watching time to read, study, and discover new interests. TV watching is a passive experience that does little to stimulate children's minds. Many parents, teachers, and other people in contact with children have observed a connection between heavy TV watching and poor school performance.

4. *Reading on a regular basis helped turn Carson's life around. Think about your daily schedule. If you were to do regular reading, where in your day could you find time to relax for half an hour and just read? What do you think would be the benefits of becoming a regular reader?*

   Answers will vary. Here are some of the benefits of being a regular reader:

   - The pleasure of losing oneself in a good story
   - The satisfaction of learning about someone or something one is interested in
   - Learning more about life and the world in general
   - Becoming an informed citizen
   - Improving one's vocabulary

SUGGESTED ANSWERS TO THE DISCUSSION QUESTIONS IN PART TWO

Note: The numbers in parentheses refer to paragraphs in the reading. Also, for some questions, additional related questions have been included to enhance class discussion.

1 WINNERS, LOSERS, OR JUST KIDS? Dan Wightman

1. *What does Wightman really mean by "winners" and "losers"? Why does the title also say, "or Just Kids"?*

   Wightman describes winners as people who succeeded academically, were attractive, and had money (1). He describes losers as those who did poorly in school (spending more time "tuning cars and drinking beer" than studying) and socially, and who enlisted in the Army instead of advancing their careers by going to a university (2). By adding "or Just Kids" to the title, Wightman suggests that "winners" and "losers" are not as fitting terms as they at first may seem to be.

2. *Were you surprised that Wightman's classmates turned out as they did? Why or why not?*

   Answers will vary.

3. *What is the meaning of the sentence "The past is fiction"? To what extent do you think it's true, if at all? In what ways* isn't *it true?*

   In writing "The past is fiction," Burroughs implies that the only important truth is what a person does from the present onward. That idea might be considered true to the extent that we overcome our pasts and build a good present and future. Yet it can be argued that there are many things in anyone's past that will always influence his or her future.

4. *Wightman writes that he "wondered why he was different, and had more luck, less guilt" than others. What factors do you suppose are involved in determining whether or not people shake their "loser's image"? What factors does Wightman name?*

   Wightman suggests that "more luck, less guilt" help a person lose a "loser's image"(13). He also suggests that not despairing, not regressing and not giving up (13) lead to success. What other factors might help someone overcome a slow start toward a successful life? Some factors to consider: goals, support, education, willpower, and the development of one's abilities.

   How might guilt keep someone from shedding a loser's image?

2 OWEN, THE STRAY CAT, Emily Carlin

1. *Carlin rolls her eyes when she hears Bob explaining to passersby why he's trying to catch the stray kitten. Do you believe Bob when he tells passersby that he's doing it because his wife told him to? Why or why not?*

   Clearly Bob prides himself on being a "dog guy" rather than a cat person. We learn that he particularly enjoys going on long walks with one of his dogs, and that he regards cats as "useless creatures" (4). Yet the fact that Bob calls his wife when he notices the stray kitten and then goes to great lengths to capture it suggests that he is more sensitive to the cat's predicament than he is willing to admit. Students should infer that Bob tells passersby that rescuing the cat is his wife's idea in order to maintain his "macho" image.

2. *Carlin mentions that she and her husband have owned a number of pets over the years. Why do you think people like Carlin and Bob like owning animals? Do you? If you do, do you prefer cats, dogs, or some other kind of pet? Explain.*

   Along with the companionship that pets provide, the satisfaction that comes with rescuing a creature in distress seems to be a major reason Carlin and Bob own so many animals. Carlin mentions that she cannot turn down a needy animal (2) and that she "couldn't have been happier" (18) when she realizes that Owen is going to make it. Although Bob tries to appear less of a "soft touch" than his wife, he clearly goes out of his way to save Owen. Additionally, the couple seem to enjoy watching their pets' behavior. Carlin describes how the other animals in the household react to Owen, while Bob likes to watch his retriever mix retrieve sticks. Other possible reasons people like owning animals could include any of the following:

   - security
   - making friends with other animal lovers
   - the pleasure or status that comes with owning a purebred animal
   - the pleasure of caring for a dependent creature
   - breeding purebred animals
   - entering animals in shows
   - the physical satisfaction that comes with petting a dog, cat or other furry animal

   Answers will vary as to what kind of pet students prefer.

3. *Even though he's not a "cat person," Bob goes to a lot of trouble to catch the kitten and bring it home. Carlin then stays up all night trying to get the kitten to eat. Have you ever had a similar experience involving rescuing and caring for an animal in distress? How far did (or would) you go to save a hurt or lost creature?*

   Answers will vary.

4. *Every year, overcrowded animal shelters are forced to "put to sleep" three to four million unwanted cats and dogs. If you were planning to adopt a cat or a dog, where would you look for one—at a breeding kennel, a pet shop, or a shelter for animals that, like Owen, have been rescued? Why would this be your choice?*

   Answers will vary. Those who prefer to adopt a purebred cat or dog would probably first look for one at a kennel or pet shop. Others, who are not particular as to breed or who like the idea of rescuing an animal, might go to an animal shelter or animal rescue program (although today purebred dogs and cats can be obtained through shelters and rescue associations such as Dalmatian Rescue, Chihuahua Rescue, Greyhound Rescue, etc).

   What are the characteristics of a responsible pet owner?

3 EYE CONTACT, Ron Clark

1. *Clark writes that he worked in fast food for "many a day." How do you think that working in the fast-food industry and in restaurants has affected his teaching?*

   Having spent "countless hours" working in the fast-food industry and in restaurants, Clark teaches his students lessons that he believes will have practical value for them in the real world. In "Eye Contact," he impresses upon his students that making eye contact is a way of indicating to others that you are serious about what you are saying, of gaining people's trust, and of showing respect. As he relates in paragraph 5, his experience waiting on restaurant and fast-food customers taught him that looking people in the eye is an important method of communicating respect. And as Clark points out in paragraph 6, when people feel respected and appreciated, they tend to work harder.

   Do you usually make eye contact with those you interact with? Why or why not?

2. *Think of a person you know who is good at making eye contact. How does that person make you feel when she or he looks you in the eye? On the other hand, do you know anyone who is bad at making eye contact? What effect does his or her inability to make eye contact have on you?*

   Students will probably agree with what Clark is saying and indicate that they feel valued when someone looks them in the eye. In addition, they will probably state that lack of eye contact makes them feel unimportant, or that the person who does not look them in the eye is untrustworthy and possibly hiding something from them.

3. *Do you think you're good at making eye contact? In what situations might it be difficult for you to make eye contact? If you had the chance, would you sign up for Clark's class? Why or why not?*

   Answers will vary. Situations where it might be difficult for students to make eye contact could include

   - speaking before an audience
   - being interviewed for a job
   - having to communicate something unpleasant or embarrassing
   - asking for a raise or a favor
   - admitting wrongdoing or apologizing
   - waiting on difficult customers

4. *Eye contact is one form of nonverbal communication—in other words, communicating to others without using words. What are some other kinds of nonverbal communication? Under what circumstances might these alternate forms of communication be even more effective than spoken words? (For one response to this question, read "Wired for Touch," page 288.)*

   Touch, of course, is one form of nonverbal communication. As Grandinetti makes clear in "Wired for Touch," touch can nonverbally communicate acceptance, friendship, respect, love, etc. Another form of nonverbal communication is body language. (See "Body Language" by Beth Johnson, page 203.) Answers to the second question will vary.

4 DISASTER AND FRIENDSHIP, Chuck Wilson

1. *Wilson was worried that the sheriff would be just "like the stereotyped image of the white Southern country sheriff." What is that image?*

   A common stereotype of a white Southern country sheriff includes these characteristics:

   - racist
   - unjust to blacks
   - unwilling to help blacks
   - anxious to get the worst possible sentences for convicted blacks

2. *Wilson asked the woman in charge at the Chester Chamber of Commerce to help him find a job. Instead, she arranged for him to get some money and his car so he could go on to Florida. Why might she have done that?*

   In writing that the woman "understood my situation" (11), Wilson implies that, among other things, she understood he was treated unfairly by some. If so, she may have wished to help counteract that unfair treatment.

   What experiences have you had or heard of in which someone helped a perfect stranger?

3. *Wilson's experience was notable partly because it showed how wrong stereotypes can be. What experiences have you had in which people did not fit their stereotypes?*

   Perhaps we have all been surprised by unexpected behavior that contradicted our preconceptions. Students' memories of such experiences can be jogged by mentioning various types of people we tend to put into boxes that they don't fit: teachers, used-car salesmen, clergypersons, older people, police officers, and racial and ethnic groups of all kinds.

4. *How do stereotypes influence our treatment of other people? What can we do to make sure we treat people as individuals, not as stereotypes?*

   Here are some questions to consider in answering:

   - Do people pick—or reject—others as friends because of their background, age, or sex, rather than because of what they really are like?
   - Are people more likely to vote for—or against—someone because of his or her age, sex, race, or ethnic background?
   - Do people tend to think that the woman in an office is a secretary? Do they tend to think that the uniformed man in a hospital is a doctor?

   Answers to the second question will vary.

5 READ ALL ABOUT IT, Fran DeBlasio

1. *Do you know anybody who has trouble reading? How does that trouble affect his or her life?*

   Answers may include the areas with which DeBlasio has had trouble, including progressing in school, finding jobs, getting a driver's license, and hiding the inability to read from others.

2. *Just how difficult is it to live in our society without being able to read? To get an idea of the answer to this question, think about your activities at home, at work or school, when shopping, in restaurants, and while driving. How much of what you do involves reading?*

   Daily reading includes the following:

   - newspapers
   - street signs
   - menus
   - recipes
   - phone books
   - written words on television, in movies, and on the Internet
   - signs identifying bus and train routes
   - store and restaurant signs
   - clothing tags telling about materials and garment care
   - lists of ingredients on cans and boxes of food.

3. *DeBlasio gives a bleak picture of the schools she attended. In what ways were your own schools like, or unlike, hers? Why do you think her teachers behaved as they did?*

   Students might consider the idea that all too often, teachers (like people in all jobs) go along with a system and avoid responsibility. In addition, they may choose the easy way out. Finally, teachers may fail to see a student's true problems or understand how to solve them.

   How can students overcome the effects of a poor education?

4. *We tend to think that people don't learn important new skills as they get older, but DeBlasio's story contradicts that idea. Describe a person or persons you know who have been able to learn new skills as they get older. What skills have these people mastered, and what character traits might be responsible for their continued progress?*

   Answers will vary but can include anyone who has learned new work skills, hobbies, etc. Students may wish to also mention people in the public eye who learned new skills. Former president Ronald Reagan, for example, learned to be a politician after a career in acting, and professional athletes often go on to new careers after their sports careers end.

6 ADULT CHILDREN AT HOME, Marilyn Mack

1. *Do you know any cases of nesting? Why did the children return home? How did it work out?*

   Answers will vary.

   Why do we assume that children should move out of their parents' homes at a certain age?

2. *Do you think today's young adults are having a harder time financially than their parents' generation? Or is the "standard of living they hoped for" higher? Or both?*

   While students may not be able to speak for "today's young adults" in general, they can discuss cases they know of, including their own. They might contrast their own standard of living with their parents' at their age. Factors to consider include where they live, how often they can afford to eat out and go to movies, and how much credit they use. They might also contrast their own economic goals with those of their parents.

3. *Mack mentions the "people who've gotten in over their heads with credit cards and utility bills." Why do you think people get into this situation? What advice would you give them?*

   Students may wish to discuss cases they know of or to speculate in general as to why people get heavily into debt.

   What can people do to avoid getting heavily into debt?

4. *Do you agree that adult children who return home, "regardless of their financial situation," should pay some room and board? If not, what financial situations should excuse adult children from paying room and board?*

   Students who feel all adult children ought to pay some room and board should present one or more reasons in support of their view. Those who disagree may wish to discuss not only the relevant financial situations but also the noneconomic ways in which adult children can contribute.

7 HOW TO MAKE IT IN COLLEGE, NOW THAT YOU'RE HERE, Brian O'Keeney

1. *What would you say is the single biggest obstacle between you and better grades? Do you need to get organized? Do you exaggerate your personal problems? How might O'Keeney's article help you overcome this obstacle?*

   Common obstacles between students and better grades:

   - Procrastination
   - Demands of friends
   - A job
   - Family obligations.

   Answers concerning how to deal with such obstacles will vary.

2. *Do you make "to-do" lists? If not, do you think you should? What are three items that you would put on your "to-do" list for today?*

   Answers will vary.

   Why do you think that writing a "to-do" list can be helpful?

3. *"Sometimes, you've just got to hang tough," O'Keeney tells us (paragraph 21). What does he mean? What are some techniques for hanging tough, instead of giving in, that have worked for you or for people you know?*

   "Hanging tough" means refusing to allow problems, no matter how real they are, to interfere with one's goals. A person who hangs tough knows that life's circumstances are sometimes difficult, but that an achiever keeps on going anyway. Techniques for hanging tough might include such things as scheduling a specific, limited time to deal with a problem, but then setting that problem aside when it's time for study. Another hang-tough technique might be to refuse to let anything short of serious illness make you miss a class—to promise yourself that no matter how upset or worried you are, you will not allow yourself to skip class.

4. *O'Keeney writes in paragraph 27, "Look at your priorities. You want a degree, or a certificate, or a career." What are* your *priorities? Explain the kind of life you hope to have and how college fits into those plans.*

   Answers will vary.

8 FALSE IDEAS ABOUT READING, Robert and Pam Winkler

1. *Which one of the myths about reading is most helpful for you to know about? How has this myth affected your reading and study habits?*

   Writing the myths on the board ("You must read every word," "Reading once is enough," "Reading has to be work") may help students focus on which is most helpful for them to know about. In discussing the myths and their relationships to reading, students may wish to differentiate between reading for school and reading for pleasure.

2. *Give an example of someone you know who has been influenced by one of the myths about reading. What could you tell this person that might change his or her attitude?*

   Students might think of a younger sibling or a friend who would benefit from knowing about one of the myths in this reading.

   Do you know of anyone who has another type of reading problem? How might that problem be solved?

3. *What do you think are the benefits of not reading every word? What are the dangers?*

   The benefits of not reading every word, according to the Winklers, are not spending time on reading that doesn't meet the purpose (3) and that doesn't interest you (5). The dangers of skimming too much are that readers may miss important points and the supporting details that make sense of main points.

4. *The Winklers write that books can "help people discover and explore parts of themselves that they may not know existed." What do they mean by this? What parts of yourself have books helped you discover and explore? Give examples from one or more books you have read.*

   To answer this question, students must focus on what they have learned about themselves from reading. Have they read a psychology text that helped to explain their feelings, reactions, and/or family situation? Have they read a short story or novel with a character that gave them insight into themselves? Or have they read a how-to publication that helped them realize they could accomplish something new?

   What do you wish you knew more about? Where might you find that information in books?

9 DEALING WITH FEELINGS, Rudolph F. Verderber

1. *What is the difference between describing feelings and displaying them? How might Doris describe her feelings to Candy after Candy says, "That first paragraph isn't very well written" (paragraph 2)?*

   Describing feelings means explaining what emotions one is feeling (8); in contrast, displaying feelings means responding to, or acting on, those feelings in some way (5). For example, take a man who has just won a lottery. First he jumps into the air and yells "Whoopee!"; then he says, "Boy, I'm feeling so happy and thrilled." First the man displayed his feelings, and then he described them.

   If Doris were to describe her feelings to Candy, she might say, "I feel very nervous when you stand over me, watch me work, and criticize my report as I'm trying to get it into shape."

2. *What do you think would be Verderber's advice on "little lies"? (See paragraph 13.)*

   Judging by paragraph 13 of the reading, Verderber would probably advise people to allow others to express how they feel without making them feel guilty. He implies that since we feel the way we do, we should be free to describe those feelings. What we do about them is another matter.

3. *Why do you think Verderber emphasizes describing feelings over the other two methods of dealing with feelings?*

   Verderber writes, "Describing is often the best strategy for dealing with feelings, not only because it gives you the best chance for a positive outcome but also, as we said, because describing feelings teaches people how to treat you" (9). We can assume that he also feels describing feelings avoids the drawbacks of the other two methods. The drawbacks of withholding feelings are possible physical and psychological problems (3); the drawback of expressing or displaying negative feelings is that interpersonal problems are created (6).

4. *What are some examples from your own experience of withholding, expressing or displaying, and describing feelings? How useful was each method?*

   To find examples of the three methods of dealing with feelings in their own lives, students can look at their family life, friendships, jobs, and classes.

10 CHILDHOOD STRESS AND RESILIENCE, Diane E. Papalia and Sally Wendkos Olds

1. *How has childhood changed since you were young? How was your own childhood different from that of your parents? What was better about your childhood as compared with childhood today? As compared with your parents' childhood? What was worse?*

   In comparing their own childhoods to those of today's children and of their parents, students might consider the following: educational and work opportunities; expectations of children; family and community values; and the national and international situations.

2. *Do you recall any experiences that you found particularly stressful as a child? If so, how did you deal with them?*

   To jog students' memories for answers to this question, the class might take another look at the box in the reading on page 517, titled "What Children Are Afraid Of." What fears did students have in regard to their parents, school, and the world? What embarrassing experiences caused them anxiety?

3. *The author states that children today are forced to grow up too quickly. What are some of the things that you believe children need time to learn and experience as children?*

   To answer this question, students might think about the best of their own childhood experiences. What childhood experiences do they especially value? Also, the class might take another look at the factors that seem to contribute to resilience (9–13). We can conclude from the list that certain experiences and relationships are desirable in childhood.

4. *Sometimes a child's healthy development is hindered by the very people who are supposed to encourage it—the child's parents, relatives, or friends. What do you believe could be done to prevent child abuse (both physical and mental)? Why do you think child abuse is so common in the United States?*

   Students will use their personal knowledge to discuss these two questions. From their discussion, a list might be compiled of the factors present in cases of child abuse (alcoholism, coming from a home with child abuse, etc.). You might also list on the board specific solutions suggested by students. Some broad categories of solutions include community support programs, educational programs in schools, and educational programs in the media.

THREE ADDITIONAL READINGS

1. CLASS PROFILES

Alex Thio

The three methods of identifying classes have been used in many studies with roughly the same result: In the United States, about 3 to 5 percent of the population are in the upper class, 40 to 50 percent in the middle class, 30 to 40 percent in the working class, and 15 to 20 percent in the poor, lower class. Sociologists disagree about the precise boundaries of these classes, but most accept these broad estimates of their sizes.

The Upper Class. Though it is a mere 3 to 5 percent of the population, the upper class possesses at least 25 percent of the nation's wealth. This class has two segments: upper-upper and lower-upper. Basically, the upper-upper class is the "old rich"—families that have been wealthy for several generations—an aristocracy of birth and wealth. Their names are in the *Social Register*, a listing of acceptable members of high society. A few are known across the nation, such as the Rockefellers, the Roosevelts, and the Vanderbilts. Most are not visible to the general public. They live in grand seclusion, drawing their incomes from the investment of their inherited wealth. In contrast, the lower-upper class is the "new rich." Although they may be wealthier than some of the old rich, the new rich have hustled to make their money like everybody else beneath their class. Thus, their prestige is generally lower than that of the old rich. The old rich, who have not found it necessary to "lift a finger" to make their money, tend to look down on the new rich.

However its wealth is acquired, the upper class is very, very rich. They have enough money and leisure time to cultivate an interest in the arts and to collect rare books, paintings, and sculpture. They generally live in exclusive areas, belong to exclusive social clubs, rub elbows with one another, and marry their own kind—all of which keeps them so aloof from the masses that they have been called the *out-of-sight class*. More than any other class, they tend to be conscious of being members of a class. They also command an enormous amount of power and influence in government and business, affecting the lives of millions.

The Middle Class. The middle class is not as tightly knit as the upper class. Middle-class people are distinguished from those above them primarily by their lesser wealth and power, and from those below them by their white-collar, nonmanual jobs.

This class can be differentiated into two strata by occupational prestige, income, and education. The *upper-middle class* consists mostly of professional and business people with high income and education, such as doctors, lawyers, and corporate executives. The *lower-middle class* is far larger in size and much more diverse in occupation. It is made up of people in relatively low-level but still white-collar occupations, such as small-business owners, store and traveling salespersons, managers, technicians, teachers, and secretaries. Though having less income and education than the upper-middle class, the lower-middle class has achieved the middle-class dream of owning a suburban home and living a comfortable life.

The Working Class. The working class consists primarily of those who have little education and whose jobs are manual and carry little prestige. Some working-class people, such as construction workers, carpenters, and plumbers, are skilled workers and may make more money than those in the lower reaches of the middle class, such as secretaries and teachers. But their jobs are more physically demanding and, especially in the case of factory workers, more dangerous. Other working-class people are unskilled, such as migrant workers, janitors, and dishwashers. There are also many women in this class working as domestics, cleaning ladies, and waitresses, and they are the sole breadwinners in their households. Because they are generally underpaid, they are often called the *working poor.*

The Lower Class. This class is characterized by joblessness and poverty. It includes the chronically unemployed, welfare recipients, and the impoverished aged. These people suffer the indignity of living in run-down houses, wearing old clothes, eating cheap food, and lacking proper medical care. Very few have finished high school. They may have started out in their youth with poorly paying jobs that required little or no skill, but their earning power began to drop when they reached their late twenties. A new lower class has emerged in recent decades: skilled workers in mechanized industry who have become unskilled workers in electronically run factories. They have first become helpers, then occasional workers, and finally the hard-core unemployed.

Most members of the lower class are merely poor. But they are often stigmatized as "the underclass," a term conjuring up images of poor people as violent criminals, drug abusers, welfare mothers who cannot stop having babies, or able-bodied men on welfare who are too lazy to work.

2. FOOD CHOICES

Eleanor Noss Whitney and Sharon Rady Rolfes

People decide what to eat, when to eat, and even whether to eat in highly personal ways, often based on behavioral or social motives rather than on awareness of nutrition's importance to health. Fortunately, many different food choices can be healthy ones, but nutrition awareness helps to make them so.

Personal Preference One reason people choose foods, of course, is that they like certain flavors. Two widely shared preferences are for the sweetness of sugar and the tang of salt. Other preferences might be for the hot peppers common in Mexican cooking or the curry spices of Indian cuisine. Some research suggests that genetics may influence people's food preferences.

Habit People sometimes select foods out of habit. They eat cereal every morning, for example, simply because they have always eaten cereal for breakfast. Eating a familiar food and not having to make any decisions can be comforting.

Ethnic Heritage or Tradition Among the strongest influences on food choices are ethnic heritage and tradition. People eat the foods they grew up eating. Every country—and every region of a country—has its own typical foods and ways of combining foods into meals.

Social Interactions Food signifies friendliness. Meals are social events, and the sharing of food is part of hospitality. Social customs almost compel people to accept food or drink offered by a host or shared by a group. When your friends are going out for pizza or ice cream, how can you refuse to go along?

Availability, Convenience, and Economy People eat foods that are accessible, quick and easy to prepare, and within their financial means. Consumers today value convenience especially highly, as reflected in their choices of meals they can prepare quickly, recipes with few ingredients, and products they can cook in microwave ovens. Many people frequently eat out or have food delivered, which limits food choices to the selections on the restaurants' menus.

Positive and Negative Associations People tend to like foods with happy associations—such as hot dogs at ball games or turkey at Thanksgiving. By the same token, people can attach intense and unalterable dislikes to foods that they ate when they felt sick, or that were forced on them when they weren't hungry. Parents may teach their children to like and dislike certain foods by using those foods as rewards or punishments.

Sometimes associations classify foods for certain uses. For example, people may believe that peanut butter is for children, or that lobster is for the rich. Then, depending on whether they permit themselves to be childlike or to indulge in luxuries, they will choose to eat or refrain from eating those foods.

Emotional Comfort Some people eat in response to emotional stimuli—for example, to relieve boredom or depression or to calm anxiety. A lonely person may choose to eat rather than to call a friend and risk rejection. A person who has returned home from an exciting evening out may unwind with a late-night snack. Eating in response to emotions can easily lead to overeating and obesity, but may be appropriate at times. For example, sharing food at times of bereavement serves both the giver's need to provide comfort and the receiver's need to be cared for and to interact with others, as well as to take nourishment.

Values Food choices may reflect people's religious beliefs, political views, or environmental concerns. For example, many Christians forgo meat during Lent, the period prior to Easter, and Jewish law includes an extensive set of dietary rules. A political activist may boycott vegetables picked by migrant workers who have been exploited. People may buy vegetables from local farmers to save the fuel and environmental costs of foods shipped in from far away. Consumers may also select foods packaged in containers that can be reused or recycled.

Body Image Sometimes men and women select certain foods and supplements that they believe will improve their physical appearances and avoid those they believe might be detrimental. Such decisions can be beneficial when based on sound nutrition and fitness knowledge, but undermine good health when based on faddism or carried to extremes.

Nutrition Finally, of course, a valid reason to select certain foods is that they will benefit health. Nutritional and health values have become influential in many consumers' food choices, even when other forces are at work. A person may choose for social reasons to go out "for pizza" with friends, but once there, might eat only one slice with a large salad of fresh vegetables. Food manufacturers have responded to scientific findings linking health with nutrition by offering an abundant selection of health-promoting foods and beverages. Consumers welcome these new foods into their diets, provided that the foods are reasonably priced, clearly labeled, easy to find in the grocery store, and convenient to prepare. These foods must also taste good—as good as the traditional choices. Of course, a person need not eat any of these "special" food to enjoy a healthy diet; ordinary foods, well chosen, serve just as well.

In summary, a person selects foods for a variety of reasons. Whatever those reasons may be, food choices influence health. Individual food selections neither make nor break a diet's healthfulness, but the balance of foods selected over time can make an important difference to health. For this reason, people are wise to allow nutrition knowledge to play a major role in their food decisions.

3. PARAPHRASING

Rudolph F. Verderber

Although it seems like common sense to ask a question to obtain additional information, most of us don't feel a need to say anything when we think we understand what a person means. Yet, serious communication problems can occur even when we believe we are certain we understand the person. Why? Because what we think a person means may be far different from what the person really means.

Paraphrasing means putting your understanding of the message into words. Paraphrasing is not mere repetition. Suppose Charley, who blew the first test, says, "I'm really going to study this time." Replying "This time you're really going to study" is mere repetition. The reply shows that you have *heard* the response but not that you have *understood* it. An effective paraphrase states the meaning received in the listener's own words. If you think Charley is talking about specific study skills, your paraphrase might be "I take it this time you're going to read and outline every chapter carefully." This statement is a paraphrase because it tells Charley the meaning you have for the words "really going to study." If your interpretation is on the mark, Charley might say "Right!" But if you have received a meaning different from what Charley intended, Charley has an opportunity to clarify the meaning with a statement such as "Well, I'm going to spend a lot more time reading chapters carefully, but I wasn't planning on outlining them." At this point, you have the chance to advance the communication by encouraging Charley to use additional study skills.

Types of Paraphrases. The meaning you get from any statement may focus on its content, the feelings represented, or both, depending on the situation. A *content paraphrase* summarizes the substantive, or denotative, meaning of the message; a *feelings paraphrase* expresses what you understand to be the emotions the person is experiencing as shown by his or her nonverbal cues.

To illustrate the difference, let's go back to Charley's statement, "I'm really going to study this time." The paraphrase "I take it this time you're going to read and outline every chapter carefully" is a content paraphrase—it focuses on the denotative meaning of the message. Depending on how Charley sounded as he spoke, an appropriate feelings paraphrase might be "So you were pretty upset with your grade on the last test." Which response is more appropriate for the situation depends on whether you perceive the emphasis of Charley's statement to be on *how* to study for a test or on his *feelings* about not doing as well as he should. Let's look at another example that contains a longer message.

"Five weeks ago, I gave the revised manuscript of my independent study to my project adviser. I felt really good about it because I felt the changes I had made really improved my explanations. You can imagine how I felt when I got the manuscript back yesterday and my adviser said she couldn't see that this draft was much different from the first."

Content paraphrase: "If I have this correct, you're saying that your adviser saw little difference, yet you think your draft was both different and much improved."

Feelings paraphrase: "You seem really frustrated that your adviser didn't recognize the changes you had made."

Of course, in real-life settings, we often don't distinguish clearly between content and feelings paraphrases; rather, we tend to use both together to give a more complete picture of the meanings we received. For instance, a combination content/feelings paraphrase of the manuscript message might well be "If I have this right, you're saying that your adviser could see no real differences, yet you think your draft was not only different but much improved. I also get the feeling that your adviser's comments really irk you."

You may be thinking that if people stated their ideas and feelings accurately in the first place, we would not have to paraphrase. Accurate wording might help us understand better, but as our study of the communication process has shown, we can seldom be sure we accurately understand what others say. Both verbal and nonverbal messages can be misunderstood; internal or external noise can interfere with our understanding; and our beliefs, assumptions, and feelings may differ from those of the speaker. Perfecting our paraphrasing ability is a significant way of improving the effectiveness of our communication.

When to Paraphrase. Common sense suggests that we wouldn't paraphrase every message we receive; nor would we paraphrase after every few sentences. Still there are times when it is important to clarify meaning before stating your own ideas or feelings. Try paraphrasing the ideas or feelings of the other person

- when you need a better understanding of a message—in terms of content, feelings, or both—before you can respond appropriately.
- when you think you understand what a person has said or how the person feels, but you're not absolutely sure.
- when you perceive that what the person has said is controversial or was said under emotional strain and, therefore, may not really be what the person meant to say.
- when you have some strong reaction to what the person has said or how the person has said it that may have interfered with your interpretation of the message.
- when you are speaking in a language that is not your native language or talking with people in a language that is not their first.

To paraphrase effectively, (1) listen carefully to the message, (2) determine what the message means to you, and (3) if you believe a paraphrase is necessary, restate the message using your own words to indicate the meaning you have received.

MODEL NOTES AND ADDITIONAL ACTIVITIES FOR "THREE ADDITIONAL READINGS"

Comments and Suggestions

- This section contains the following for each of the three additional reading selections on pages 43–48 of this *Instructor's Manual*:
  1. An outlining or mapping activity.
  2. The completed outline or map of the reading. These outlines and maps can be copied and distributed for comparison purposes after students have completed the activity or taken their own notes.
  3. A short quiz on the reading, which can be copied and given after students have finished taking notes on the reading. The quizzes will demonstrate to students how much they have learned simply through good notetaking. (Answers to the three quizzes are on page 60.)
- The three readings can be assigned one at a time throughout the semester after students have worked through "Supporting Details," Chapter 4 in Part One, in which outlining and mapping are explained.
- I suggest assigning the readings in terms of level of difficulty. From easiest to hardest, I would sequence the readings as follows:

  Food Choices (easiest)
  Class Profiles
  Paraphrasing (hardest)
- Following are some notetaking guidelines you may wish to copy and pass out and/or briefly go over with students.

Some Notetaking Guidelines

- Before beginning to take notes, carefully read through and mark the material.
- Here's how to mark material: Circle definitions, set off examples with an *Ex,* and underline or bracket ideas that seem especially important. Use numbers (1, 2, 3 . . .) to mark off major items in a series.
- Then take notes by writing down each heading in turn and listing the important ideas that you find under that heading. Think carefully about each heading; it is often a key to main ideas and major details.
- Keep outlines simple. Often just one level of symbols (1, 2, 3 . . .) will do.
- Sometimes you may want two levels, and they can be labeled as follows:

  1.
     a.
     b.
  2.
     a.
     b.

MAPPING ACTIVITY: "CLASS PROFILES"

The Four Social Classes in the U.S.

	Members (% of population; financial and work characteristics)	Lifestyle characteristics
Upper class	3-5% of pop. and at least 25% of wealth Upper-upper: live on interest of inherited wealth; ex.: Rockefellers Lower-upper: ____________________ __________________________________	Time, money to enjoy and collect art; live in exclusive areas and socialize w/each other; have great power and influence in gov't and business
Middle class	40-50% of population—not as wealthy as upper class, but not in manual jobs of lower class Upper-middle class: _____________ __________________________________ _______________________ Exs.: doctors, lawyers, executives Lower-middle class— _____________ __________________________________ __________________________________ __________________________________ __________________________________	Own suburban home, live a comfortable life
Working class	__________________________________ __________________________________ Skilled workers—may make more money than lower-middle class workers Exs: construction workers, plumbers __________________________________ __________________________________ __________________________________	(no details given in reading)
Lower class	15-20% of population—"the underclass" The chronically unemployed, welfare recipients, poor aged, skilled factory workers who became unskilled in electronically-run factories	__________________________________ __________________________________ __________________________________

A MAP OF "CLASS PROFILES"

The Four Social Classes in the U.S.

	Members (% of population; financial and work characteristics)	Lifestyle characteristics
Upper class	3-5% of pop. and at least 25% of wealth Upper-upper: live on interest of inherited wealth; ex.: Rockefellers Lower-upper: had to work for their money	Time, money to enjoy and collect art; live in exclusive areas and socialize w/each other; have great power and influence in gov't and business
Middle class	40-50% of population—not as wealthy as upper class, but not in manual jobs of lower class Upper-middle class: more prestige, income, and education then lower-middle class. Exs.: doctors, lawyers, executives Lower-middle class—larger in size, more diverse in occupation than upper-middle class. Exs.: small-business owners, salespersons, teachers, secretaries	Own suburban home, live a comfortable life
Working class	30-40% of population; in manual job without prestige Skilled workers—may make more money than lower-middle class workers Exs: construction workers, plumbers Unskilled workers—"the working poor" Examples: migrant workers, janitors, dishwashers	(no details given in reading)
Lower class	15-20% of population—"the underclass" The chronically unemployed, welfare recipients, poor aged, skilled factory workers who became unskilled in electronically-run factories	Run-down housing, old clothes, cheap foods, poor medical care

A QUIZ ON "CLASS PROFILES"

Check what you've learned in taking notes on "Class Profiles" by filling in each blank with the letter of the matching description.

_____ Lower-upper class	A.	Includes the "working poor"
_____ Upper-middle class	B.	Marked by joblessness and poverty
_____ Lower-middle class	C.	Very rich with self-earned money
_____ Working class	D.	Includes teachers and salespersons
_____ Lower class	E.	Made up of professional and business people with high income and education

OUTLINING ACTIVITY: "FOOD CHOICES"

Complete the following outline.

Reasons for food choices:

1. ______________________________—people like certain flavors; genetics may be a factor.
2. ___________________—no decision to make; eat cereal in morning because always have.
3. _______________________________—every country and region has its own typical foods.
4. Social interactions—eating is a way to be part of a group; for example, _______________

   ____
5. Availability, convenience, and economy—people eat foods that are accessible, quick, and easy and affordable to prepare
6. Positive and negative associations—positive example is ____________________________

   ______________________________; negative example is food a child is made to eat as punishment.
7. ____—people may eat to relieve boredom, depression, or anxiety.
8. Values—food choices may reflect religious beliefs (no meat during Lent), political views (boycotting vegetables picked by migrant workers), or environmental concerns (vegetables grown by local farmers to save fuel costs).
9. _____________________________________—choosing foods based on whether they will improve or harm physical appearance.
10. Nutrition—choosing foods to benefit health; for example, __________________________

    ____

AN OUTLINE OF "FOOD CHOICES"

Reasons for food choices:

1. Personal preferences—people like certain flavors; genetics may be a factor.
2. Habit—no decision to make; eat cereal in morning because always have.
3. Ethnic heritage or tradition—every country and region has its own typical foods.
4. Social interactions—eating is a way to be part of a group; for example, going out for pizza with friends.
5. Availability, convenience, and economy—people eat foods that are accessible, quick, and easy and affordable to prepare
6. Positive and negative associations—positive example is turkey at Thanksgiving; negative example is food a child is made to eat as punishment.
7. Emotional comfort—people may eat to relieve boredom, depression, or anxiety.
8. Values—food choices may reflect religious beliefs (no meat during Lent), political views (boycotting vegetables picked by migrant workers), or environmental concerns (vegetables grown by local farmers to save fuel costs).
9. Body image—choosing foods based on whether they will improve or harm physical appearance.
10. Nutrition—choosing foods to benefit health; for example, eating large salad along with slice of pizza.

A QUIZ ON "FOOD CHOICES"

Check what you've learned in taking notes on "Food Choices" by answering the following questions.

____ 1. Which sentence expresses the main idea of the selection?

A. In choosing which foods to eat, people should put nutrition needs ahead of personal preference.

B. While people choose foods for a variety of reasons, nutrition awareness should play a role as well.

C. Most people have various positive and negative associations with certain foods.

____ 2. Overeating and obesity often result when people eat

A. for emotional comfort.

B. foods with negative associations.

C. for body image.

____ 3. Eating restaurant food

A. is always unhealthy.

B. is usually cheaper than eating homemade food.

C. limits food choices.

____ 4. People eat foods out of habit because familiar foods

A. are nutritious.

B. tend to be cheaper.

C. require no decisions and are comforting.

____ 5. People can find nutritious foods among

A. many new foods.

B. many ordinary foods.

C. both of the above.

OUTLINING ACTIVITY: "PARAPHRASING"

Complete the following outline of the selection.

Paraphrasing is a way to make a message clear by putting your understanding of it into words.

Two types of paraphrases (which can be used separately or together):

1. Content paraphrase: summarizes the meaning of the words
2. Feelings paraphrase: ____

____

When to paraphrase:

1. When you need a better understanding of a message, in terms of content and/or feelings
2. ____.
3. When you think what was said is not what the person meant to say because of its controversial nature or the person's emotional strain
4. ____.
5. ____.

Steps to paraphrasing effectively:

1. Listen carefully to the message.
2. ____.
3. If you believe a paraphrase is necessary, restate the message to show the meaning you have received.

AN OUTLINE OF "PARAPHRASING"

Paraphrasing is a way to make a message clear by putting your understanding of it into words.

Two types of paraphrases (which can be used separately or together):

1. Content paraphrase: summarizes the meaning of the words
2. Feelings paraphrase: expresses what you understand the person's emotions to be, based on nonverbal clues

When to paraphrase

1. When you need a better understanding of a message, in terms of content and/or feelings
2. When you think you understand but you're not sure
3. When you think what was said is not what the person meant to say because of its controversial nature or the person's emotional strain
4. When your own strong reaction might have interfered with your interpretation
5. When the language being spoken is not your or the speaker's first language

How to paraphrase

1. Listen carefully to the message.
2. Determine what it means to you.
3. If you believe a paraphrase is necessary, restate the message to show the meaning you have received.

A QUIZ ON "PARAPHRASING"

Check what you've learned in taking notes on "Paraphrasing" by answering the following questions.

____ 1. Paraphrasing means
- A. putting your understanding of someone else's message into words.
- B. putting your own message into words.
- C. listening very carefully to someone else's message.

____ 2. A feelings paraphrase
- A. summarizes the meaning of someone's words.
- B. expresses what you understand to be the emotions behind a message.
- C. expresses your own feelings about another person's message.

____ 3. TRUE OR FALSE? A content paraphrase and a feelings paraphrase should never be used together.

____ 4. One good time to paraphrase is
- A. after every message that is received.
- B. after every few sentences of a message that is received.
- C. when you have a strong reaction to what the person has said.

____ 5. The first step in paraphrasing a message is to
- A. try to guess what the message will be.
- B. listen carefully to the message.
- C. decide what the message means to you.

ANSWERS TO THE QUIZZES ON THE THREE ADDITIONAL READINGS

Quiz on "Class Profiles"

C lower-upper class
E upper-middle class
D lower-middle class
A working class
B lower class

Quiz on "Food Choices"

1. B
2. A
3. C
4. C
5. C

Quiz on "Paraphrasing"

1. A
2. B
3. F
4. C
5. B

TEST BANK

This section contains the following:

- A **Test Bank** (pages 63–150) consisting of four additional mastery tests for each chapter in Part One of *Ten Steps to Building College Reading Skills*, Fifth Edition, as well as four additional Combined-Skills Mastery Tests;
- An **answer key** (pages 151–155) to the 44 tests in the test bank.

Instructors whose students are using *Ten Steps to Building College Reading Skills*, Fifth Edition, in class have permission to reproduce any of these tests on a photocopying machine (or a secure website) as often as needed.

Name ______________________________

Section ______________ Date ___________

SCORE: (Number correct) × 5 = _________%

DICTIONARY USE: Test A

A. Below are five pairs of dictionary guidewords followed by a series of other words. Circle the **two** words in each series that would be found on the page with the guidewords.

1–2. **earth science / echo**

earthworm   each   easy   earthquake   eel

3–4. **glib / gloom**

gist   glide   gloat   goatee   glossy

5–6. **hiccup / high-rise**

hippopotamus   hide-out   hockey   horseradish   hi-fi

7–8. **roar / roll**

roadrunner   rock 'n' roll   romantic   roger   rookie

9–10. **thunderhead / tide**

termite   throb   Thursday   tidy   tiddlywinks

B. Use your dictionary and the spelling hints on page 41 of the textbook to find the correct spellings of the following words.

11. occupashun ______________________________
12. canser ______________________________
13. errer ______________________________
14. millitary ______________________________
15. mistery ______________________________

(Continues on next page)

C. Use the pronunciation key to answer the questions below.

Pronunciation Key

ă **h**a**t**	ā **p**a**y**	âr **c**a**re**	ä **c**a**rd**	ĕ **t**e**n**	ē **sh**e	ĭ **s**i**t**
ī **h**i	îr **h**e**re**	ŏ **l**o**t**	ō **g**o	ô **a**ll	oi **oil**	ou **out**
o͝o **l**oo**k**	yo͝o **c**u**re**	o͞o **c**oo**l**	yo͞o **u**se	ŭ **up**	ûr **f**u**r**	th **th**ick
th **th**en	ə **a**go, it**e**m, eas**i**ly, gall**o**p, circ**u**s					

16. The *e* in *cell* (sĕl) is pronounced like the *e* in what common word? ________________

17. The *y* in *ruby* (ro͞o′bē) is pronounced like the *e* in what common word? ________________

18. The *a* in *Mars* (märz) is pronounced like the *a* in what common word? ________________

19. The *u* in *dumpling* (dŭmp′lĭng) is pronounced like the *u* in what common word? ________________

20. The *u* in *immunity* (ĭ-myo͞o′nĭ-tē) is pronounced like the *u* in what common word? ________________

Name ______________________

Section ____________ Date ____________

SCORE: (Number correct) × 5 = ________%

DICTIONARY USE: Test B

A. Place dots between the syllables in the following words. Then write the correct pronunciation symbols, including the accent marks. Use your dictionary.

1. m a r k e t ______________________
2. z i p p e r ______________________
3. f r a c t u r e ______________________
4. d i m i n i s h ______________________
5. p e s t i c i d e ______________________

B. Answer the questions about the four words below. The pronunciation key on page 40 of the textbook will help you answer some of the questions.

choir (kwīr)	**log•ic** (lŏj′ĭk)
in•ven•tion (ĭn-vĕn′shən)	**moon•struck** (mo͞on′strŭk′)

6. Which **two** words have the sound of *i* as in *sit*?

   ______________________ ______________________

7. Which word has the sound of *o* as in *lot*? ______________________
8. Which word has the schwa sound? ______________________
9. Which word has a primary and secondary accent? ______________________
10. Which words have two syllables? ______________________

C. Use your dictionary to list the parts of speech for the following words.

11. reason ______________________
12. cool ______________________
13. one ______________________
14. under ______________________
15. advance ______________________

(Continues on next page)

D. Use your dictionary to write the irregular plural forms for the following words.

16. volcano ______________________

17. family ______________________

18. half ______________________

19. tooth ______________________

20. mouse ______________________

Name ______________________________
Section ____________ Date ____________
SCORE: (Number correct) × 5 = ________%

DICTIONARY USE: Test C

A. Answer the questions that follow the dictionary entries. The pronunciation key below will help you answer the pronunciation questions.

Pronunciation Key

ă hat	ā pay	âr care	ä card	ĕ ten	ē she	ĭ sit
ī hi	îr here	ŏ lot	ō go	ô all	oi oil	ou out
o͝o look	yo͝o cure	o͞o cool	yo͞o use	ŭ up	ûr fur	th thick
th then	ə ago, item, easily, gallop, circus					

ar•row (ăr′ō) *n.* **1.** A straight, thin shaft that is shot from a bow and usually made of light wood with a pointed head at one end and flight-stabilizing feathers at the other. **2.** Something similar to an arrow in form, function, or speed. **3.** A sign or symbol shaped like an arrow and used to indicate direction.

_____ 1. The *a* in *arrow* is pronounced like the *a* in
A. *hat.*
B. *pay.*

_____ 2. The *o* in *arrow* is pronounced like the *o* in
A. *lot.*
B. *go.*

_____ 3. *Arrow* is accented on
A. the first syllable.
B. the second syllable.

_____ 4. Which definition best fits the sentence below—definition 1, 2, or 3?

To reach Pizza Palace, take the first right after the intersection, and then follow the *arrows* to the parking lot.

_____ 5. Which definition best fits the quotation below—definition 1, 2, or 3?

I shot an *arrow* in the air,
It fell to earth, I knew not where.
—*Henry Wadsworth Longfellow*

(Continues on next page)

di•vert (dĭ-vûrt′ *or* dī-vûrt′) *v.* **-vert•ed, -vert•ing, -verts.** **1.** To turn aside from a course or direction. **2.** To distract or draw one's attention. **3.** To give pleasure by distracting the attention from worries; amuse. **—di•vert′er** *n.* **—di•vert′ing•ly** *adv.*

_____ 6. Which guidewords would be on the dictionary page with *divert*?

A. **disturb / diversity**
B. **ditzy / divide**
C. **divest / divulge**

_____ 7. How many ways can the *i* in *divert* be pronounced?

A. One
B. Two
C. Three

_____ 8. How many syllables does the adverb form of *divert* have?

A. One
B. Two
C. Three
D. Four

_____ 9. Which definition of *divert* fits the sentence below—definition 1, 2, or 3?

Texting while driving is dangerous—it will *divert* the driver's attention and is likely to cause an accident.

_____10. Which definition of *divert* fits the sentence below—definition 1, 2, or 3?

The policeman *diverted* the traffic onto a side street until the tow truck had removed the broken-down bus.

B. Use your dictionary and the spelling hints on page 41 of the textbook to find the correct spellings of the following words.

11. seazon ______________________________
12. believible ______________________________
13. emerjancy ______________________________
14. governer ______________________________
15. indiferant ______________________________

C. Place dots between the syllables in the following words. Then write the correct pronunciation symbols, including the accent marks. Use your dictionary.

16. n i f t y ______________________________
17. f r u g a l ______________________________
18. f o r f e i t ______________________________
19. f e a t h e r b r a i n ______________________________
20. s t e r e o t y p e ______________________________

Name ______________________________

Section ______________ Date ___________

SCORE: (Number correct) × 5 = ________%

DICTIONARY USE: Test D

A. Answer the questions that follow the dictionary entries. The pronunciation key below will help you answer the pronunciation questions.

Pronunciation Key

ă **hat**	ā **pay**	âr **care**	ä **card**	ĕ **ten**	ē **she**	ĭ **sit**
ī **hi**	îr **here**	ŏ **lot**	ō **go**	ô **all**	oi **oil**	ou **out**
o͝o **look**	yo͝o **cure**	o͞o **cool**	yo͞o **use**	ŭ **up**	ûr **fur**	th **thick**
th **then**	ə **ago, item, easily, gallop, circus**					

flop (flŏp) *v.* **flopped, flop•ping, flops** **1.** To fall or lie down heavily and noisily. **2.** To move about loosely or limply. **3.** *Informal.* To fail completely. **4.** *Slang.* To go to bed. *—n.* **1.** The sound made when flopping. **2.** *Informal.* A complete failure.

_____ 1. How many definitions does the verb form of *flop* have?
A. One
B. Two
C. Three
D. Four

_____ 2. Which guidewords would be on the dictionary page with *flop*?
A. **flower / fly**
B. **flock / Florida**
C. **flirt / flog**

_____ 3. In the sentence below, the definition of *flop* that applies is
A. verb definition 1.
B. verb definition 2.
C. noun definition 1.
D. noun definition 2.

The TV show was a *flop*; the network canceled it after the second week.

_____ 4. In the sentence below, the definition of *flop* that applies is
A. verb definition 1.
B. verb definition 2.
C. verb definition 3.
D. noun definition 1.
E. noun definition 2.

After the long walk in the hot sun, the exhausted dog staggered into the kitchen and *flopped* on the cool floor.

_____ 5. In the sentence below, the definition of *flop* that applies is
A. verb definition 2.
B. verb definition 3.
C. verb definition 4.
D. noun definition 1.
E. noun definition 2.

The clown's baggy pants were so long that the cuffs *flopped* around his huge shoes as he walked.

(Continues on next page)

mod•er•ate (mŏd′ər-ĭt) *adj.* **1.** Within reasonable limits; not excessive. **2.** Not subject to extremes; mild or calm. **3.** Opposed to radical or extreme views, especially in politics or religion. —*v.* (mŏd′ə-rāt′) **-at•ed, -at•ing, -ates** **1.** To become less violent, severe, or extreme. **2.** To preside over or act as chairman of.

_____ 6. The *a* in the adjective *moderate* is pronounced like
A. the *i* in *sit*. B. the *i* in *hi*. C. the *a* in *hat*.

_____ 7. The *a* in the verb *moderate* is pronounced like the *a* in
A. *hat*. B. *pay*. C. *card*.

_____ 8. Which syllable has the strongest accent in the verb form of *moderate*?
A. The first B. The second C. The third

_____ 9. In the sentence below, the definition of *moderate* that applies is
A. adjective definition 1.
B. adjective definition 2.
C. adjective definition 3.
D. verb definition 1.
E. verb definition 2.

We've had high winds and bitterly cold temperatures for the past five days, but the newspaper says we will have more *moderate* weather by the end of the week.

_____10. In the sentence below, the definition of *moderate* that applies is
A. adjective definition 1.
B. adjective definition 2.
C. adjective definition 3.
D. verb definition 1.
E. verb definition 2.

The TV anchorman was asked to *moderate* the first of the televised debates between the two presidential candidates.

B. Use your dictionary to write the irregular plural forms for the following words.

11. hero ______________________ 13. calf ______________________

12. city ______________________ 14. sister-in-law ______________________

C. Using your dictionary, write the pronunciation and meaning of the boldfaced word in each sentence. Make sure that you choose the definition that best fits the sentence.

15–16. "I'm rather **partial** to broccoli," Uncle Rick said, as he helped himself to his third serving.
A. Pronunciation: ______________________
B. Definition: ______________________

17–18. The company **sandbagged** the employees into working overtime by threatening to fire them.
A. Pronunciation: ______________________
B. Definition: ______________________

19–20. I had expected my grandmother's eighty-ninth birthday party to be pretty **tame**, but it turned out to be the wildest celebration I'd ever been to.
A. Pronunciation: ______________________
B. Definition: ______________________

Name ______________________________
Section ______________ Date ___________
SCORE: (Number correct) × 10 = ________%

VOCABULARY IN CONTEXT: Test A

A. For each item below, underline the **examples** that suggest the meaning of the italicized word. Then, in the space provided, write the letter of the meaning of that word.

___ 1. Joan loves to buy *exotic* foods: vegetables and herbs from China, spices from India, olives from Greece, and cheeses from France.
A. Chinese
B. healthy
C. common
D. foreign

___ 2. Unskilled workers must often take jobs that are *tedious,* such as washing dishes for hours or flipping burgers day after day.
A. dangerous
B. requiring great strength
C. boring
D. rare

___ 3. Emotionally disturbed people may be troubled by *morbid* thoughts. For instance, they may often think about suicide or murder.
A. busy
B. shy
C. depressing
D. practical

B. Each item below includes a word or words that are a **synonym** of the italicized word. Write the synonym of the italicized word in the space provided.

____________________ 4. Barry was *ecstatic* when Lynda agreed to marry him. He was so overjoyed that he burst out singing on his way home.

____________________ 5. *Rituals* are a common and important part of life. These ceremonies include marriages and funerals.

C. Each item below includes a word or words that are an **antonym** of the italicized word. Underline the antonym of each italicized word. Then write the letter of the meaning of the italicized word.

___ 6. A flashing yellow light means "slow down," but many drivers *accelerate* instead, trying to get through the intersection before the light turns red.
A. reverse direction
B. stop
C. take a detour
D. speed up

___ 7. "I'm willing to *affirm* that I was present when the crime was committed," the witness said. "But I strongly deny that I took part in it."
A. guess
B. state as true
C. predict
D. forget

(Continues on next page)

D. Use the **general sense of each sentence** to figure out the meaning of each italicized word. Then write the letter of the meaning of the italicized word.

___ 8. An old saying is still true—"Be nice to people as you *ascend* the ladder of success. You may meet them again later, on your way down."

A. watch
B. go up
C. fall off
D. go down

___ 9. The Navy *bestowed on* the admiral its highest honor.

A. gave to
B. demanded of
C. took away from
D. asked of

___10. Gail and Jon don't always see eye to eye—for instance, they have *contrary* opinions about religion and politics. But still, they're a happy couple.

A. opposing
B. weak
C. the same
D. strong

Name ______________________________

Section ______________ Date ____________

SCORE: (Number correct) × 10 = ________%

VOCABULARY IN CONTEXT: Test B

A. For each item below, underline the **examples** that suggest the meaning of the italicized word. Then, in the space provided, write the letter of the meaning of that word.

___ 1. A *pessimist* expects bad news in every letter, an F on every test, and a "no" to every request.

A. someone careless
B. someone hopeful
C. someone who expects the worst
D. a dreamer

___ 2. The mental patient had two *delusions.* He believed that someone was plotting against him. He also thought that he was being controlled by something put into his brain.

A. desires
B. false beliefs
C. illnesses
D. habits

B. Each item below includes a word or words that are a **synonym** of the italicized word. Write the synonym of the italicized word in the space provided.

____________________ 3. "Even when I make a perfectly simple statement," the politician complained, "the newspapers *distort* my meaning. They always twist my words."

____________________ 4. Attempts are being made to *fortify* the Leaning Tower of Pisa in Italy. The authorities believe they must strengthen the tower to prevent it from eventually falling down.

____________________ 5. Dr. Fell is a strong *advocate* of acupuncture. He is also a strong supporter of herbal remedies.

C. Each item below includes a word or words that are an **antonym** of the italicized word. Underline the antonym of each italicized word. Then write the letter of the meaning of the italicized word.

___ 6. Many people who suffer from shyness have a fear of being *conspicuous.* They dress in dull, quiet clothing in order to be almost unnoticeable.

A. weak
B. attracting attention
C. unattractive
D. happy

___ 7. Dawn cooked such an *elaborate* dinner for her friends that she had to work nonstop in the kitchen. If she had planned a simple menu, she could have relaxed and spent more time with her guests.

A. delicious
B. healthful
C. expensive
D. complicated

(Continues on next page)

8. "We have no time for on-the-job training here," the interviewer told Chung. "So we can't hire a *novice.* We need an expert with plenty of experience."

   A. someone with a college degree   C. beginner
   B. someone who isn't a citizen   D. retired person

D. Use the **general sense of each sentence** to figure out the meaning of each italicized word. Then write the letter of the meaning of the italicized word.

___ 9. The efforts of the firemen to save the woman were *futile*—she was already dead.

   A. successful   C. useless
   B. early   D. too lengthy

___10. The saying "Never put off till tomorrow what you can do today" warns that it is best not to *procrastinate.*

   A. delay   C. rush
   B. work too hard   D. confuse

Name ______________________
Section ___________ Date ___________
SCORE: (Number correct) × 10 = ________%

VOCABULARY IN CONTEXT: Test C

Using context clues for help, write the letter of the best meaning for each italicized word.

___ 1. In Dickens's *A Christmas Carol,* the *miserly* Ebenezer Scrooge is visited by three spirits who change him into a generous man.
A. stingy
B. kind
C. wise
D. insane

___ 2. During the flood, people who had to leave their homes found *refuge* in the school gym, where they stayed for two days.
A. answers
B. flooding
C. shelter
D. towels

___ 3. To get their ideas across, textbook authors often use tables, charts, and graphs. These visual aids are an effective way to *convey* complicated information.
A. create
B. conceal
C. ignore
D. communicate

___ 4. At first, the surgery seemed to be successful. But several hours later, the patient's condition began to *deteriorate,* and it continued to worsen over the next days.
A. improve
B. get worse
C. stay the same
D. become clear

___ 5. If you're trying to give up smoking, here's a tip: Don't have any cigarettes readily *accessible.* Instead, put them all far out of reach.
A. within reach
B. affordable
C. acceptable
D. low tar

___ 6. The two towns are *comparable* in size; they both have a population of about twenty thousand. They are also very much alike in terms of average income.
A. contrasting
B. in competition
C. similar
D. unusual

___ 7. "I turn off the TV when there's a news story about a *gruesome* murder," Patrick said. "I don't want my kids to be frightened by all the gory details."
A. recent
B. probably untrue
C. little-known
D. horrible

___ 8. *Optimists* are likely to work hard because they believe it is possible to reach high goals.
A. one who expects disappointment
B. one who is always puzzled
C. one who works hard
D. one who expects good things

(Continues on next page)

___ 9. In addition to his vacation, Victor can take off three "personal days." But this extra time off can be taken only for a *legitimate* reason, such as a medical emergency or a meeting with a child's teacher.

A. health
B. proper
C. secret
D. old

___10. A famous *anecdote* about Mark Twain illustrates his sense of humor: When a newspaper announced that he had died, he sent a telegram saying, "Reports of my death are greatly exaggerated."

A. biography
B. prediction
C. brief story of an event
D. amusing riddle

Name ______________________

Section ____________ Date ____________

SCORE: (Number correct) × 10 = ________%

VOCABULARY IN CONTEXT: Test D

Using context clues for help, write the letter of the best meaning for each italicized word.

___ 1. When you are first trying to ice skate, you may seem hopelessly *inept.* But don't give up—with practice and patience, you will learn to skate.

A. unskilled
B. talented
C. confident
D. uninterested

___ 2. The interest in plays seems to be *universal.* Theater has developed in every culture in the world.

A. unimportant
B. intelligent
C. quite rare
D. found everywhere

___ 3. *Stereotypes* are not just racial or ethnic. Consider, for instance, the "dumb blond," the hot-tempered redhead, and the jolly fat person.

A. facts
B. languages
C. groups
D. oversimplified images

___ 4. It's a mistake to assume that if two events are *consecutive,* the first must have caused the second. For instance, Thursday does not cause Friday, and spring does not cause summer.

A. happening at the same time
B. happening unexpectedly
C. happening one after the other
D. happening daily

___ 5. In a research paper, you must *cite* your sources. You can present them in footnotes or endnotes, or in parentheses within the text itself.

A. increase
B. make known
C. find
D. remove

___ 6. Raul is an *indulgent* father. For instance, he lets his daughter stay up as late as she likes and never insists that she does her homework.

A. seeking advice
B. giving in to someone's wishes
C. absent often
D. strict

___ 7. People with red-green color blindness cannot *discriminate* between reds and greens. People with blue-yellow color blindness cannot distinguish between blues and yellows.

A. prefer
B. care
C. paint
D. tell the difference

___ 8. Both children and adults sometimes purposely act less *competent* than they really are. By pretending to be helpless, they can get others to do things for them.

A. trusting
B. capable
C. nervous
D. friendly

(Continues on next page)

___ 9. "Necessity is the mother of invention" is an old saying. It means that when a need exists, creative minds will *devise* something to meet that need.

A. buy
B. invent
C. hide
D. oppose

___10. Languages *evolve* over time, as you can see if you open a page of *The Canterbury Tales,* written about six hundred years ago by the English poet Chaucer. It is barely recognizable as English today.

A. remain the same
B. improve
C. develop and change
D. get worse

Name ______________________
Section ____________ Date ____________
SCORE: (Number correct) × 4 = ________%

MAIN IDEAS: Test A

A. Each cluster of words below is made up of a general idea and four specific ideas. The general idea includes all of the specific ideas. Underline the general idea in each group.

1. local news	TV program	game show	situation comedy	reality show
2. chocolate	raspberry	lemon	butterscotch	flavor
3. button	zipper	Velcro	fastener	snap
4. actor	entertainer	dancer	singer	comedian
5. mother	father	son	granddaughter	family
6. love	hate	anger	emotion	joy
7. road	boulevard	freeway	turnpike	expressway

B. In each item below, one idea is general and the others are specific. The general idea includes the specific ones. In the spaces provided, write in two more specific ideas that are covered by the general idea.

8. *General:* apartment problems
Specific: no hot water, broken lock, ______________, ______________

9. *General:* means of transportation
Specific: boat, airplane, ______________, ______________

10. *General:* fruit
Specific: orange, banana, ______________, ______________

11. *General:* dog
Specific: pit bull, collie, ______________, ______________

12. *General:* time to give a gift
Specific: Valentine's Day, anniversary, ______________, ______________

13. *General:* language
Specific: English, Latin, ______________, ______________

14. *General:* question word
Specific: who, where, ______________, ______________

15. *General:* long-term goal
Specific: get a degree, learn French, ______________, ______________

(Continues on next page)

C. In each pair below, one idea is general and the other is specific. The general idea includes the specific one. Do two things:

a Underline the idea in each pair that you think is more general.
b Then write in one more specific idea that is covered by the general idea.

16. punishment	hanging	__________
17. honey	sweetener	__________
18. river	body of water	__________
19. exercise	sit-up	__________
20. chore	washing dishes	__________
21. cough syrup	medicine	__________
22. difficult weather	tornado	__________
23. oak	wood	__________
24. seasoning	pepper	__________
25. symptom	cough	__________

Name ______________________________

Section ______________ Date __________

SCORE: (Number correct) × 5 = ________%

MAIN IDEAS: Test B

A. Each cluster of words below is made up of a general idea and four specific ideas. The general idea includes all of the specific ideas. Underline the general idea in each group.

1. chapter	book	index	cover	table of contents
2. rose	daisy	tulip	flower	carnation
3. comforters	sheets	bedding	blankets	pillowcases
4. expense	food	taxes	gas	rent
5. turtle	reptile	crocodile	snake	alligator
6. elbow	wrist	joint	knee	ankle
7. oxygen	hydrogen	neon	gas	carbon monoxide
8. novelist	poet	playwright	writer	journalist

B. (9–20.) In each group below, one statement is the general point, and the other statements are specific support for the point. Identify the point with a **P** and each statement of support with an **S.**

Group 1

_____ My parents complain when I come home late.

_____ I think it's time for me to look for my own apartment.

_____ My mother wants detailed information about all the people in my life.

_____ My parents want me to start paying rent for living at home.

Group 2

_____ We can go weeks without food, but only two or three days without water.

_____ Water is needed for the body to wash away its waste products.

_____ Water is essential to the human body.

_____ Water also moistens the body's tissues so they can carry oxygen.

(Continues on next page)

Group 3

_____ The economy is in a slump.

_____ At present, unemployment is especially high.

_____ The real estate market is down, but people still can't afford to buy homes.

_____ Many individuals and businesses have filed for bankruptcy.

Name ______________________________

Section ______________ Date ___________

SCORE: (Number correct) × 5 = _________%

MAIN IDEAS: Test C

A. In each pair below, one idea is general and the other is specific. The general idea includes the specific one. Do two things:

a Underline the idea in each pair that you think is more general.
b Then write in one more specific idea that is covered by the general idea.

1. flounder	fish	______________________
2. amount	pound	______________________
3. outerwear	wool scarf	______________________
4. yogurt	dairy product	______________________
5. sofa	furniture	______________________
6. fictional character	Cinderella	______________________

B. (7–10.) In the following group, one statement is the general point, and the other statements are specific support for the point. Identify the point with a P and each statement of support with an S.

_____ The biggest female stars make less money than the most famous male stars.

_____ Very few good roles are written for older women.

_____ The film industry tends to treat women as second-class citizens.

_____ Only a handful of women have been allowed to direct major motion pictures.

C. (11–18.) Each group of items below includes one topic, one main idea (topic sentence), and two supporting details. In the space provided, label each item with one of the following:

T—for the topic
MI—for the main idea
SD—for the supporting details

Group 1

_____ Young Amish boys learn to help their fathers tend crops and livestock.

_____ Amish children are taught to assist their parents with family work.

_____ The children in Amish families.

_____ Amish girls are taught to help their mothers cook, clean, and sew.

(Continues on next page)

Group 2

_____ Lloyd's of London's insurance policies.

_____ Bruce Springsteen had his voice insured for $6 million.

_____ One model was insured against developing "worry lines" on her face.

_____ Lloyd's of London has sold some odd insurance policies.

D. Read the passage below and then answer the questions that follow.

[1]To describe the business of marketing, we can use the A-T-R theory. [2]According to that theory, there are three stages in selling a product: Awareness, Trial, and Reinforcement. [3]The first stage, awareness of a product, is achieved through advertising. [4]To bring about the second stage, the trial, many companies give away free samples or coupons. [5]Finally, reinforcement involves constantly reminding the consumer to try the product again.

_____ 19. The list words that signal the main idea of the paragraph are
A. *the A-T-R theory.*
B. *three stages.*
C. *free samples or coupons.*

_____ 20. The addition words that introduce the major details of the paragraph are
A. *business, theory, selling.*
B. *according, the, to bring about.*
C. *first, second, finally.*

Name ____________________

Section __________ Date __________

SCORE: (Number correct) × 10 = ______%

MAIN IDEAS: Test D

A. (1–4.) The following group of items includes one topic, one main idea (topic sentence), and two supporting details. In the space provided, label each item with one of the following:

T—for the topic
MI—for the main idea
SD—for the supporting details

_____ The ancient Aztecs of Mexico.

_____ The Aztecs practiced bloody human sacrifice, but they also valued such gentle arts as poetry.

_____ The Aztecs were fierce soldiers, but they were also skilled farmers who knew how to bring water to the desert and how to grow crops on wetlands.

_____ The Aztec culture included surprising contradictions.

B. Write the letter of the correct topic of each of the following paragraphs. Then find the sentence in which the author states the main idea about that topic, and write that number in the space provided.

Paragraph 1

[1]John Fitzgerald Kennedy was made for television. [2]His tall, thin body gave him the strong vertical line that cameras love, and his weatherbeaten good looks appealed to women and men. [3]He had a full head of hair, and even in the winter he maintained a tan. [4]In addition, he was always "cool" in public. [5]This too was tailor-made for the "cool medium," television. [6]Wit, irony, and understatement, all delivered casually, translate well on television.

___ 5. The topic is
A. politicians.
B. John F. Kennedy.
C. President Kennedy's wit.

___ 6. Write the number of the sentence that states the main idea of the paragraph.

(Continues on next page)

Paragraph 2

[1]In 1801, a candidate for Congress challenged to a duel an Army officer who called him "a bowl of skimmed milk." [2]At that duel, the two men killed each other. [3]Newspaper editors were challenged so often that many put on their pistols when they dressed in the morning. [4]In Vicksburg, Mississippi, three newspaper editors died in duels in the 1840s. [5]These examples indicate that as recently as the 1800s, dueling with weapons was a common way to defend one's honor.

___ 7. The topic is
- A. ways to defend one's honor.
- B. newspaper editors' dueling to defend their honor.
- C. dueling to defend one's honor.

___ 8. Write the number of the sentence that states the main idea of the paragraph.

Paragraph 3

[1]Shakespeare wrote that "all the world's a stage." [2]He meant that everyone has at least one part, or role, to play in life. [3]In fact, every role we play has an "on stage" and a "backstage" area; in the first area, we're on our best behavior; but in the second area, we can "let our hair down." [4]For example, in the dining room, a waiter is "on stage." [5]No matter how rushed he is or how annoyed he feels, a waiter is expected to be polite and helpful to his customers. [6]Once he returns to the kitchen, however, it's another matter. [7]There he is "backstage" and can let his true feelings show. [6]In the kitchen, the waiter can make sarcastic remarks about the customers or even joke about serving a plate of food that's been dropped.

___ 9. The topic is
- A. "on stage" and "backstage" roles.
- B. human behavior.
- C. "backstage" behavior.

___10. Write the number of the sentence that states the main idea of the paragraph.

Name ______________________
Section ____________ Date ____________
SCORE: (Number correct) × 10 = ________%

SUPPORTING DETAILS: Test A

A. (1–5.) Complete the outline below by filling in the missing major details. Then answer the question that follows the outline.

[1]Research suggests ways in which parents can encourage creativity in children. [2]One way is to provide a stimulating environment. [3]As much as possible, the environment should be designed to match a child's special interests and talents. [4]Second, teach by focusing on a child's strengths. [5]Avoid criticizing his or her weaknesses. [6]Another important method is to encourage nonconforming behavior. [7]You can do this by helping your children avoid or resist peer pressure. [8]Fourth, set an example by pursuing interesting work or intellectual or artistic hobbies. [9]Finally, do not use rigid control over children. [10]Children who are constantly directed seem to lose the confidence needed for the creative spirit.

Main idea: Research suggests ways in which parents can encourage creativity in children.

1. ______________________________
2. ______________________________
3. Encourage nonconforming behavior.
4. ______________________________
5. ______________________________

5. What words in the main idea tell us that a list is coming?

____

(Continues on next page)

B. (6–10.) Complete the map by finishing the heading and filling in the missing major details. Then answer the questions that follow the map.

[1]Several different factors influence people's eating habits. [2]Personal preference is one of the most important factors that determines what people eat. [3]Almost all people enjoy the sweetness of sugar and the tang of salt. [4]Others like spices, such as the hot peppers common in Mexican food or the curry usually found in Indian dishes. [5]Another factor that influences eating is culture. [6]People often like to eat the foods they grew up eating. [7]And every country—and region of a country—has its own special foods and ways of combining foods into meals. [8]Economics is a third issue that affects what and how people eat. [9]Foods that are readily available at low cost often become part of people's diets. [10]Likewise, meals made with expensive or hard-to-get ingredients are rarely eaten, if at all.

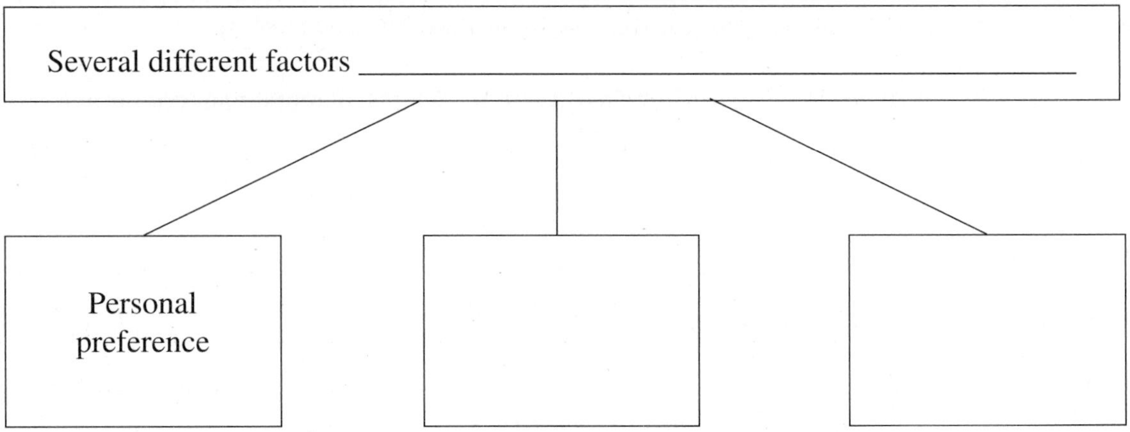

9. What addition word introduces the second major detail? ______________________

10. What addition word signals the third major detail? ______________________

Name ______________________

Section ____________ Date ____________

SCORE: (Number correct) × 10 = ________%

SUPPORTING DETAILS: Test B

A. (1–4.) Complete the outline below by filling in the major details. Include brief explanations for each, as shown for the first major detail.

[1]Three broad types of leadership have been identified. [2]First is the autocratic style. [3]The autocratic leader centralizes authority and does not involve others in decision making. [4]This manager uses authority in a straightforward manner. [5]He or she simply issues orders. [6]A second type of leader is the democratic leader. [7]The democratic leader shares authority and involves employees in decision making. [8]He or she encourages employee participation and communication. [9]At the same time, this type of leader makes it clear that he or she has the final say. [10]Finally, the "hands off" leader leads by taking the role of consultant. [11]He or she provides encouragement for employees' ideas and offers insights or opinions when asked.

Main idea: Three broad types of leadership have been identified.

1. ______________________________—simply issues orders.

2. ______________________________
   ____

3. ______________________________
   ____

4. What word or words in the main idea tell us that a list is coming?

   ____

(Continues on next page)

B. (5–10.) Fill in the major details and examples needed to complete the map below. Then answer the questions that follow the map.

[1]The common concerns or points of view that people share are called interests, and the groups that organize them are called interest groups. [2]There are two general types of interest groups. [3]One is special interest groups. [4]They are groups that mainly seek benefits from which their members would gain more than the society as a whole. [5]Examples include chambers of commerce, trade associations, labor unions, and farm organizations. [6]The second type of interest group is public interest groups. [7]These are groups which pursue policies that are thought to be of no greater benefit to their members than to the larger society. [8]Consumer protection organizations are good examples of public interest groups.

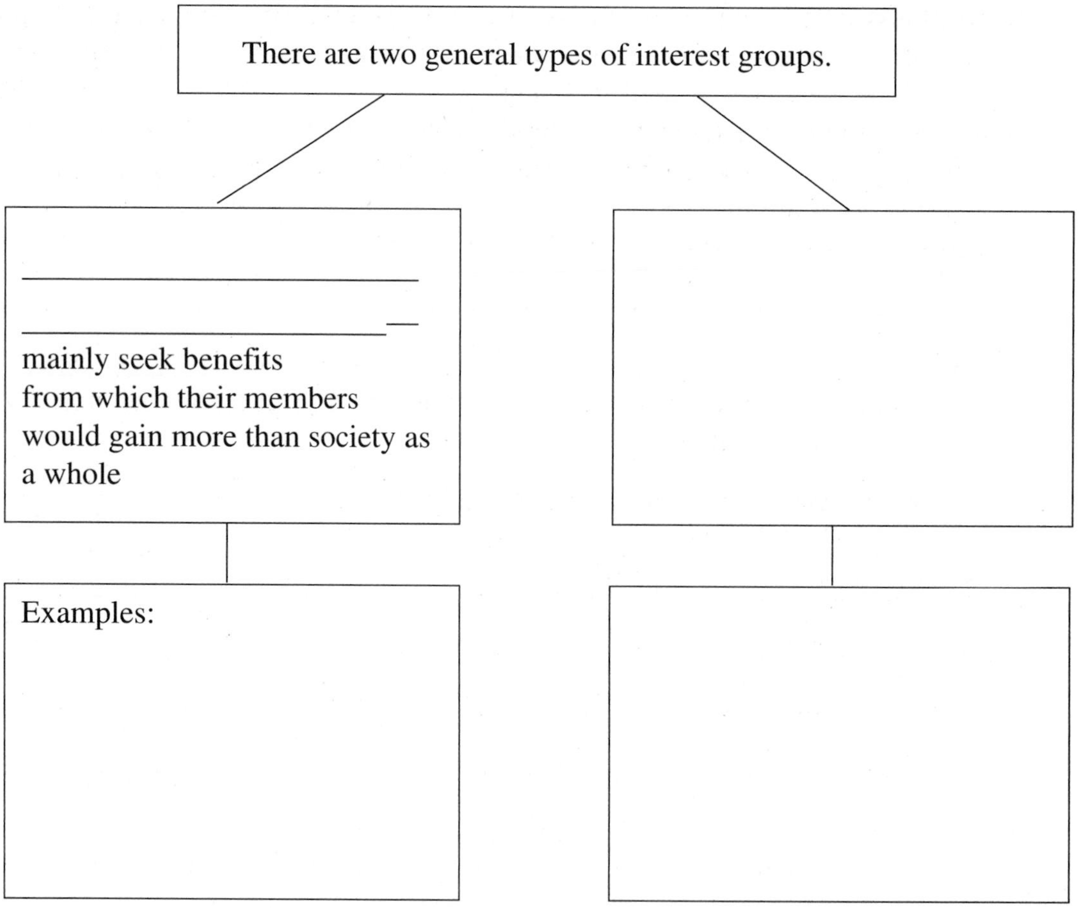

9. What addition word introduces the first major detail? ______________

10. What addition word introduces the second major detail? ______________

Name ______________________________
Section ______________ Date ___________
SCORE: (Number correct) × 10 = ________%

SUPPORTING DETAILS: Test C

A. (1–6.) Complete the outline below by filling in the missing major and minor details. Some details have been filled in for you. (You may find it helpful to mark off with a check or number the major details in the paragraph.)

[1]Having to give a speech or report in front of a group of other people can be a frightening experience, but there are ways you can make it more bearable. [2]One way to reduce your fear is to choose a topic you know something about and are interested in. [3]If you are comfortable with your topic, you will feel more relaxed when you are in front of an audience. [4]You will also have more confidence in your ability to say something worthwhile on a topic you care about. [5]A second key in controlling nervousness is to prepare well for your speech. [6]Take time to organize your points so your audience can learn what you want them to know. [7]Also, rehearse your speech several times so you will feel confident you know it well. [8]A third way to deal with your fear is to practice relaxation activities just before it is time to deliver your speech. [9]On the day of your speech, try to clear your mind, telling yourself you have done all you can to prepare yourself. [10]Then, as you approach the speaker's stand, take a deep breath and smile, reminding yourself that in a few minutes your speech will be over.

Main idea: There are ways to make giving a speech more bearable.

1. Choose a topic ______________________________.
   a. Feeling more comfortable with your topic will make you feel more relaxed in front of an audience.
   b. You will also have more confidence in your ability to say something worthwhile on a topic you care about.
2. ______________________________
   a. ______________________________
   b. ______________________________
3. ______________________________
   a. ______________________________
   b. As you approach the speaker's stand, take a deep breath, smile, and remind yourself that in a few minutes, your speech will be over.

(Continues on next page)

B. (7–10.) Complete the main idea and fill in the major details needed to complete the map below.

[1]The level of stress in working parents can be high. [2]Professionals, however, offer several suggestions on how to help keep the demands of home and job in balance. [3]First of all, set limits. [4]This means to set aside time to relax and enjoy yourself. [5]Another helpful suggestion is to make frequent lists of things to do in the order of importance you give them. [6]At the top of the list may be "spend time with my children" and "go to work"; at the bottom may be "return Dora's call." [7]A third suggestion to fight stress is to ask for help. [8]Tell your spouse, partner, or children exactly what you want from them. [9]Discuss ways to share responsibilities at home. [10]It is also helpful to team up with other parents to share chores such as child care and driving kids to school. [11]Finally, say the experts, don't aim for perfection—perfection is an obstacle to reducing stress. [12]For instance, be willing to tolerate less-than-perfect results on household chores.

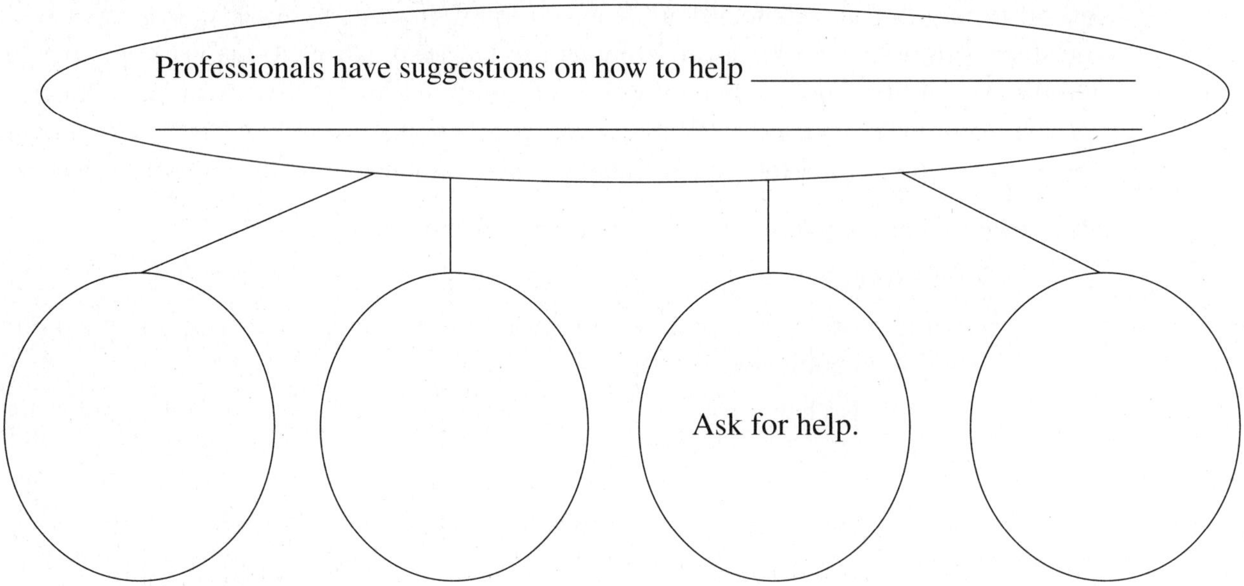
Professionals have suggestions on how to help ______________________
____
Ask for help.

Name ______________________________

Section ______________ Date ____________

SCORE: (Number correct) × 10 = ________%

SUPPORTING DETAILS: Test D

A. (1–6.) Complete the outline below by filling in the missing major and minor details. Some details have been filled in for you. (You may find it helpful to mark off with a check or number the major details in the paragraph.)

[1]Once a virus, bacteria, or other pathogen enters your body, you can go through the five stages of a disease. [2]First is the incubation period, which begins once the disease-causing agent enters your body. [3]During this time, the pathogens multiply and spread throughout your body. [4]Next is the early-symptom stage. [5]During this stage, the disease is highly contagious. [6]Symptoms are usually general and mild. [7]They can include fever, headache, sneezing and tiredness. [8]The third stage, clinical disease, is the peak of the disease. [9]Specific symptoms of the disease usually appear. [10]For example, jaundice is a symptom of hepatitis. [11]Swelling of the face along the jawbone is a symptom of mumps. [12]Because symptoms develop that a doctor can observe, the disease can usually be diagnosed during this stage. [13]Symptoms begin to disappear in the decline stage. [14]Although you start to feel better, your body is still weakened from the disease. [15]You can become worse if you become too active too soon. [16]Sometimes you can still transmit the disease to others during this stage. [17]Convalescence is the final stage during which your body recovers. [18]Most diseases are not contagious during convalescence.

Main idea: Once a virus, bacteria, or other pathogen enters your body, you can go through the five stages of a disease.

1. Incubation period
   a. It begins once the disease-causing agent enters your body.
   b. Pathogens ______________________________
2. Early-symptom stage
   a. ______________________________
   b. Symptoms are usually general and mild.
3. Clinical disease
   a. This is the peak of the disease.
   b. Specific symptoms of the disease usually appear, allowing doctor to diagnose the illness.
4. ______________________________
   a. You start to feel better, but are still weak and can become worse if you become too active.
   b. ______________________________
5. ______________________________
   a. Your body recovers during this stage.
   b. ______________________________

(Continues on next page)

B. (7–10.) Fill in the major details and the one missing explanation needed to complete the map below.

[1]There are three common ways people respond to those who offend or bother them. [2]Perhaps the most common way people deal with such negative situations is through passive behavior. [3]Passive people do not share their feelings when they are upset. [4]Instead of trying to stop what is bothering them, passive people will often remain silent and allow others to continue their annoying behavior. [5]A second way people deal with a negative situation is through aggressive behavior. [6]Aggressive people lash out at those who have hurt them—with little regard for others' feelings. [7]The third way of dealing with negative situations is through assertive behavior. [8]Like those who are aggressive, assertive people also actively address the cause of their problem—they just do it differently. [9]They don't yell at the person who has bothered them. [10]Instead, assertive people will discuss what has annoyed them and then work to find a way to fix it.

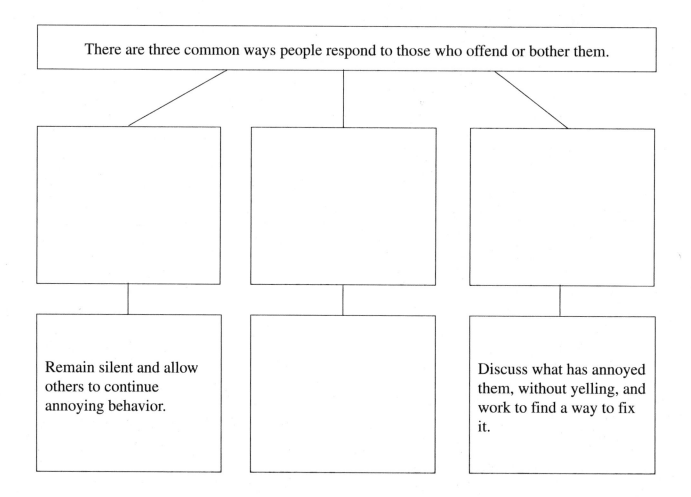

There are three common ways people respond to those who offend or bother them.

Remain silent and allow others to continue annoying behavior.		Discuss what has annoyed them, without yelling, and work to find a way to fix it.

Name ______________________________

Section ______________ Date ___________

SCORE: (Number correct) × 20 = ________%

LOCATIONS OF MAIN IDEAS: Test A

The main idea may appear at any place within each of the five paragraphs that follow. Write the number of each main idea in the space provided.

___ 1. [1]A character in a novel or a short story may be older or younger than you. [2]The character may live on a farm, while you live in a city. [3]The character may be living long ago—during the American Revolution, or in ancient Rome, or in the Middle Ages. [4]The character may be male while you are female, white while you are black, rich while you are poor—or vice versa. [5]Rarely do you meet a fictional character who is just like yourself, so when you read fiction, you must step outside the narrow boundaries of your own life.

___ 2. [1]Behavior experts think there are two main reasons why some people experience stress when buying clothes for themselves. [2]First, anxious shoppers often don't like the look of their bodies, and trying on clothes (especially in front of mirrors) makes them confront what they'd rather not think about. [3]Second, these people are sometimes unsure about what image they want to project (studious? sexy? respectable?), so it's hard for them to make clothing choices without feeling frustrated.

___ 3. [1]Blocking out your feelings may seem like a good way to protect yourself at emotionally difficult times. [2]But psychologists report that people who keep feelings locked inside are likely to run into trouble. [3]First, unexpressed emotions only deepen and become even more troubling. [4]Also, people with buried emotions often have a difficult time relating to others and are afraid of being hurt if they open up. [5]In addition, those hidden feelings may eventually find a harmful way to get out. [6]For example, people whose feelings are blocked off are more likely to have alcohol problems, attempt suicide, or try to hurt others.

___ 4. [1]Few things are more boring than standing in line. [2]Luckily, some ways have been found to make waiting in line more bearable. [3]Airline personnel now use hand-held devices to look up customers' information, scan or print boarding passes, and direct passengers to the appropriate area. [4]One New York bank pays five dollars to any customer who has waited more than five minutes. [5]Fast-food restaurants have found that timing the work of fast-food workers motivates crews to work more quickly, resulting in lines that move faster. [6]Dividing tasks so that one person takes an order while another begins to prepare it also gets food to customers more quickly. [7]In amusement parks, customers complain less when signs explain how long people can expect to wait. [8]Also, live entertainment such as a magician or juggler cheers people waiting in long lines.

(Continues on next page)

___ 5. [1]Wording with more than one meaning can unnecessarily confuse and disappoint. [2]For instance, unclear language on a menu resulted in a disappointed diner. [3]The menu listed "tostada with beans." [4]The customer, expecting a tostada with beans on the side, was disappointed to be served a tostada with beans inside of it. [5]A more serious misunderstanding occurred when a nurse told one of her patients that he "wouldn't be needing" his robe, books, and shaving materials anymore. [6]The patient became quiet and moody. [7]When the nurse asked about the odd behavior, she discovered that the poor man had interpreted her statement to mean he was going to die soon. [8]In fact, the nurse meant he would be going home shortly.

Name ______________________

Section ____________ Date ____________

SCORE: (Number correct) × 20 = ________%

LOCATIONS OF MAIN IDEAS: Test B

The main idea may appear at any place within each of the five paragraphs that follow. Write the number of each main idea in the space provided.

___ 1. [1]By having a device called a teletypewriter, or TTY, deaf people can communicate on the telephone using the written word rather than the voice. [2]Two people with this equipment converse by dialing the phone number in the usual way. [3]Then they type out their message on the keyboard of the TTY. [4]The message is transmitted over the telephone line and gets printed out on a screen or paper, depending on the type of TTY used. [5]The receiver can then type back a message to the original caller, and so on.

___ 2. [1]Why do people go to the theater? [2]Of course, there are all sorts of individual answers to this question. [3]In general, though, theatergoers seem to have three main motives: to be entertained, to join in a shared experience, and to stretch their minds. [4]Entertainment is probably the most typical reason: most people go to a play to relax and enjoy themselves. [5]Sharing an experience is also significant. [6]At a live performance, people come together and form a group, almost a little community. [7]The third reason is important to many audience members: for them, theater is a way of enriching the mind and learning something, a source of personal growth.

___ 3. [1]In the seventeenth century, the Dutch became very fond of collecting tulip bulbs. [2]The finest bulbs gained high prices, and traders began making a profit in buying and selling them. [3]Eventually, people paid great fortunes for single tulip bulbs, kept them for a few weeks, and then sold them for even a higher price. [4]But finally, buyers realized that the bulbs were not worth the high prices demanded. [5]The great Tulip Mania came to a sudden end when prices fell greatly overnight. [6]Interest in the common Dutch tulip thus led to one of the first "crashes" in economic history.

___ 4. [1]You can help save the Earth by forming some environmentally sound habits. [2]Store foods in covered bowls instead of wrapping them in foil. [3]Write on both sides of a piece of paper, and use scrap paper for messages. [4]Turn off the water—until you need it—while washing dishes, brushing your teeth, or shaving. [5]Eliminate a couple of car trips per week. [6]Choose cloth diapers instead of disposable ones. [7]Avoid lawn-care chemicals, which can find their way into water supplies. [8]Also, put aluminum cans, plastic containers, and papers in recycling containers when you are finished with them.

(Continues on next page)

___ 5. [1]People who are convicted of robbing or burglarizing strangers are likely to be sent to prison. [2]But policemen and prosecutors tend to regard crimes between acquaintances less seriously than other crimes. [3]For example, suppose that Joe and Dan know each other. [4]Dan steals Joe's TV set, and claims he did it because Joe didn't pay back money that Dan had lent him. [5]This is likely to be regarded as a sort of private matter—Joe may not be considered altogether innocent by the police and prosecutor. [6]And Dan is less likely to be sent to prison than if he had stolen the TV from someone he didn't know.

Name ______________________

Section ____________ Date ____________

SCORE: (Number correct) × 20 = ________%

LOCATIONS OF MAIN IDEAS: Test C

The main idea may appear at any place within each of the five paragraphs that follow. Write the number of each main idea in the space provided.

___ 1. [1]If a naked woman rode down your street on a horse, could you resist taking a look? [2]That's the decision a tailor in Coventry, England, had to make in the eleventh century. [3]The governor of his town was making the people pay too much in taxes. [4]The governor's wife, Godiva, asked him to have mercy on the people. [5]He agreed to be more merciful if she would ride through the streets naked, and that's what Lady Godiva did. [6]All the people in town covered their windows so that they would not embarrass the lady. [7]But one tailor, Tom, took a look. [8]And so ever since Lady Godiva's naked ride, the term "peeping Tom" has meant someone who watches people secretly.

___ 2. [1]Children who are neglected or abused in early childhood can be damaged to a degree that can never be fully repaired. [2]One little girl known as Anna is a sad example. [3]Anna was the child of a young unmarried woman living in a rural area in the 1940s. [4]The child's mother confined her to a dark attic room, where she was given enough milk to live, but almost no human contact. [5]When Anna was 6, she was discovered by the authorities and placed in a foster home. [6]At that time, she appeared to be deaf and profoundly mentally retarded, being unable to walk, talk, or even chew. [7]Eventually Anna began to learn to walk and talk, but she never achieved anything approaching normal development. [8]Her early malnutrition led to her death at age 11.

___ 3. [1]A conflict can exist only when both parties are aware of a disagreement. [2]For instance, you may be upset for months because a neighbor's loud stereo keeps you awake at night, but no conflict exists between the two of you until the neighbor learns of your problem. [3]Of course, you can communicate your displeasure with somebody without saying a word. [4]A dirty look, the silent treatment, or avoiding the other person are all ways of expressing yourself.

___ 4. [1]Before the 1840s, schools were quite limited in terms of the numbers who attended and the quality of education. [2]Apprenticeship was a major form of education. [3]Formal schooling was largely available to those who could afford to pay. [4]Even "free" schools often required the payment of tuition. [5]And primary schools often required entering students to already be able to read. [6]This policy kept out students who had not been taught to read by their parents. [7]Many schools admitted pupils regardless of age, mixing young children with young adults. [8]Classrooms could contain as many as eighty pupils. [9]Few textbooks were available, and most learning amounted to monotonous repetition of facts. [10]School buildings were generally unpainted, overcrowded, and lacked chalkboards or windows.

(Continues on next page)

___ 5. [1]Over the ages, many cultures have considered it better to be right-handed than left-handed. [2]And it is true that being left-handed has disadvantages, such as being more prone to allergies. [3]However, left-handedness does have advantages. [4]Benjamin Franklin, Leonardo da Vinci, and Pablo Picasso were all left-handed. [5]All these men (males are more likely than females to favor the left hand) had a highly developed ability to visualize space. [6]That ability is a quality that may be stronger in left-handed people. [7]This fact may explain the high proportion of left-handed architects. [8]Also, left-handed people may actually be more likely to have special intellectual gifts. [9]A study of over 100,000 twelve- and thirteen-year-olds found nearly 300 who scored very high on the Scholastic Aptitude Test (SAT). [10]Twenty percent of this top-scoring group were left-handed, twice the rate of left-handedness in the general population.

Name ______________________________

Section ______________ Date ___________

SCORE: (Number correct) × 20 = ________%

LOCATIONS OF MAIN IDEAS: Test D

The main idea may appear at any place within each of the five paragraphs that follow. Write the number of each main idea in the space provided.

___ 1. [1]In African cultures, music is a very important part of life, with many functions. [2]Music is used for entertainment, for dancing, in plays, and in ceremonies. [3]It also marks specific life events such as birth, coming of age, marriage, and death. [4]Music often accompanies work, with special songs for, say, chopping wood, rowing a boat, and harvesting crops. [5]There are even special songs for when people are suing each other in a law court. [6]And music is also a way of communicating—songs are used to pass on a group's history and to report and comment on current news.

___ 2. [1]In naturally stressful situations, the time of greatest stress is not necessarily the time when danger is at its height. [2]This fact is illustrated by a research study of the pattern of stress on a group of twenty-eight parachutists. [3]Each man was asked to describe his feelings before, during, and after his jump. [4]All reported an increase of fear and of desire to escape as the time for the jump approached. [5]Once the men were in line and realized that they could not turn back, however, they began to calm down. [6]By the time they reached the most dangerous part of the jump—when they were in free fall and waiting for their chutes to open—they had calmed down.

___ 3. [1]When you're embarrassed or ashamed, your face turns red. [2]When you're frightened, you grow pale. [3]Both blushing and turning pale are the result of activity in your nervous system. [4]Certain nerves react to your emotional state. [5]Those nerves in turn affect the tiny blood vessels in your face and neck. [6]When those vessels grow larger, allowing more blood to flow through them, you blush. [7]When they become smaller, the blood supply is lessened. [8]Then you grow pale.

___ 4. [1]Have you ever wondered why some animals, including human beings, walk upright instead of on all fours? [2]For one thing, bipedalism—walking on two feet rather than four—makes an animal taller and thus able to see farther. [3]This helps the animal to spot danger and food or water sooner. [4]Also, a taller animal can stretch higher for foods, such as eggs in birds' nests or nuts and fruits growing on trees. [5]Second, bipedalism frees the front limbs for use as arms and hands rather than as legs and and feet; this means that the animal can grasp and carry objects and, most important, use tools. [6]Thus walking on two feet has important advantages for well-being and even survival.

(Continues on next page)

___ 5. [1]A sole proprietorship is a business owned by one person. [2]It is one of the most common forms of business ownership. [3]Sole proprietorship has both advantages and disadvantages. [4]One advantage is ease of starting. [5]All you have to do to begin a sole proprietorship is to obtain any necessary licenses, open your doors, and start selling your goods or services. [6]Once you're under way, you have the satisfaction of working for yourself. [7]You can make your own decisions—what hours to work, whom to hire, what prices to charge, and so on. [8]Best of all, you can keep all the profits, assuming there are any. [9]However, sole proprietorships are usually quite small since a single person's financial resources are likely to be limited. [10]Furthermore, sole proprietors are financially fully responsible for their businesses. [11]They may even have to sell their family home to satisfy a business debt.

Name ______________________

Section ____________ Date ____________

SCORE: (Number correct) × 10 = ________%

RELATIONSHIPS I: Test A

A. Fill in each blank with the appropriate transition word or words from the box. Use each transition once. Then, in the space provided, write the letter of the transition you have chosen.

A. after	B. another	C. first
D. in addition	E. later	

___ 1. [1]Francis Scott Key wrote "The Star-Spangled Banner" in 1814. [2](He took the melody from an eighteenth-century drinking song). [3]Over a century ________________, in 1931, the song was adopted as the national anthem by the United States Congress.

___ 2. [1]Before reading your first assignment in a textbook, acquaint yourself with the format and content of the book. [2]________________, read the table of contents. [3]Next, skim the book, looking for ways the author organizes information and highlights important points.

___ 3. [1]Birds make certain sounds to communicate with their young. [2]They also make calls that signal the presence of food. [3]________________, birds cry out alarms to warn their flock to take to the air.

___ 4. [1]Leaders have several qualities. [2]Surveys have found that most formal leaders are above average in height. [3]________________ common quality of leaders is enthusiasm.

___ 5. [1]A well-known psychologist suggested that humans seek to satisfy a series of needs, including those for food, sleep, and spirituality. [2]Higher-level needs can be fulfilled only ________________ the more basic ones have been met.

(Continues on next page)

B. Fill in each blank with one of the transitions in the box. Use each transition once. Then answer the question that follows.

after	finally	one
second		

[1]Have you ever had trouble remembering information despite hours of studying? [2]This trouble may make your studying a frustrating experience. [3]However, there are a number of methods you can use to improve your memory—and your test scores. [4](6)____________________ method is to overlearn information. [5]This means that (7)____________________ you feel that you really know the material, you should still review it one to three more times. [6]A (8)____________________ good method is to organize and categorize information. [7]Many students take notes on class material but fail to organize it into more easily learned lists or steps. [8](9)____________________, you should interact in some way with the information you have learned. [9]For example, if you take notes on and outline a biology chapter, you will understand and remember it better than if you had just tried to memorize parts of it.

____10. The main pattern of organization of the above paragraph is
- A. list of items.
- B. time order.

Name ____________________

Section ____________ Date ____________

SCORE: (Number correct) × 10 = ________%

RELATIONSHIPS I: Test B

A. Write the letter of the answer that describes the relationship indicated by the italicized transition.

___ 1. *During* a tornado, winds can reach over one hundred miles an hour.

The relationship of the two parts of the sentence is one of
A. addition. B. time.

___ 2. [1]In April 1961, the Russians launched the first manned satellite. [2]Less than a month *later,* on May 5, 1961, American Alan B. Shepard was sent into space for a fifteen-minute flight.

The relationship of the second sentence to the first is one of
A. addition. B. time.

___ 3. [1]There are several ways to save money on your weekly grocery bill. [2]First, look for sales. [3]Next, clip and use coupons. [4]*Third,* buy as many items as you can in large economy sizes.

The relationship of the last sentence to the previous sentences is one of
A. addition. B. time.

___ 4. *After* the Civil War, there were no laws to protect the consumer from false claims for ineffective or even dangerous medicines.

The relationship of the two parts of the sentence is one of
A. addition. B. time.

___ 5. [1]To make your writing more clear, use words that your readers are likely to understand. [2]*Also,* use transitions to help your reader understand the relationships between ideas.

The relationship of the second sentence to the first sentence is one of
A. addition. B. time.

B. Read the passage and then answer the question that follows.

[1]Most people would agree that the more variety there is in a fireworks display, the better. [2]There are actually four different types of fireworks available. [3]The first type, skyrockets, explode high in the air and produce the most dramatic effects. [4]These are the fireworks that are most likely to produce "oohs" and "aahs" from the crowd. [5]The next type, Roman candles, shoot out separate groups of sparks and colored flames. [6]This display is accompanied by a series of loud booming noises. [7]The third type, pinwheels, throw off sparks and flames as they whirl on the end of a stick. [8]Finally, lances are thin, colorful fireworks used in ground displays.

___ 6. The main pattern of organization of the above paragraph is
A. list of items.
B. time order.

(Continues on next page)

C. Fill in each blank with the appropriate transition word from the box. Use each transition once. Then answer the question that follows.

during	final	next

[1]A supervisor must sometimes counsel employees about certain long-term practices that must change for the good of the company. [2]Such problems include drug abuse, frequent errors, and tardiness. [3]There are four stages in the process of counseling employees. [4]The first stage is identifying the problem. [5](7)____________________ this stage, the supervisor helps the employee identify and explain a problem and its causes. [6]The second stage is seeing how determined the employee is. [7]If he or she shows little or no interest in solving the problem, it's time to consider removing that person from the organization. [8]If, however, the employee shows some desire to solve the problem, then the supervisor should move on to the (8)____________________ stage. [9]Stage three is solving the problem. [10]The problem will be solved more effectively if the employee is involved in creating and evaluating methods of correction. [11]The (9)____________________ stage is following up on the solution. [12]The supervisor and employee meet again at a specified time to review the results of their action plan. [13]If the situation has improved, then praise or some other reward is in order. [14]If it has not changed or has worsened, then the next meeting must once again emphasize the problem and its consequences.

____10. The main pattern of organization of the above paragraph is
A. list of items.
B. time order.

Name ______________________

Section ____________ Date ____________

SCORE: (Number correct) × 10 = ________%

RELATIONSHIPS I: Test C

Read each textbook passage and answer the questions or follow the directions provided.

A. [1]A psychologist has identified three elements in attitudes. [2]The first element is beliefs. [3]They are your basic values. [4]For example, if good health is one of your values, you probably believe people should exercise. [5]The second element of attitudes is emotions. [6]Emotions are what separate attitudes from opinions. [7]Suppose someone asked a woman if she thought colleges should have books on earthquakes. [8]She replies, "Sure," and then goes on with her daily activities. [9]Her opinion is pro-education, but she does not have any emotions about knowledge of earthquakes. [10]However, if she became upset about the lack of library books on earthquakes, her opinion would be developing into an attitude. [11]Because attitudes and emotions go together, there is almost always some form of behavioral result, so the third element of attitudes is behavior. [12]For example, if you feel strongly about an issue, you might write a letter or contribute to a campaign.

___ 1. The main pattern of organization of the above selection is
A. list of items.
B. time order.

2–3. Two of the transitions that signal major details of the paragraph are
____________________ and ____________________.

B. [1]Cardiopulmonary resuscitation (CPR) is a simple technique involving just a few steps. [2]First, open the victim's mouth and be certain that the mouth, nose and throat are free of any obstructions. [3]Then begin artificial breathing by blowing into the victim's mouth while keeping the nostrils closed with your fingers. [4]Next, check to see if there is a pulse. [5]Finally, if there is no pulse, begin a rhythmic pumping action on the chest over the heart to restore circulation.

___ 4. The main pattern of organization of the above selection is
A. list of items.
B. time order.

5. The words that introduce the major supporting details of the passage are *first, then,*
____________________, and *finally.*

(Continues on next page)

C. [1]We generally think of listening as a single activity. [2]However, there are four different types of listening. [3]The first type is appreciative listening. [4]It is done for pleasure or enjoyment, such as when we listen to music or a comedy routine. [5]The second type is empathic listening, which provides emotional support for the speaker, such as when we lend an ear to a friend in need. [6]The third type, comprehensive listening, is used to understand the message of a speaker. [7]This type of listening occurs, for example, when we attend a classroom lecture or listen to directions to find a friend's house. [8]The final type of listening is critical listening, which we use to evaluate a message for acceptance or rejection. [9]We use critical listening when we judge the sales pitch of a used-car dealer or the campaign speech of a political candidate.

___ 6. The main pattern of organization of the above paragraph is

A. list of items.

B. time order.

7–10. Complete the outline of the paragraph by finishing the main idea and filling in or completing the major details.

There are four different ______________________________

1. ______________________________—for pleasure or enjoyment

2. Empathic listening—to provide emotional support for the speaker

3. ______________________________

4. ______________________________—to evaluate a message to either accept or reject it

Name ____________________

Section ____________ Date ____________

SCORE: (Number correct) × 10 = ________%

RELATIONSHIPS I: Test D

Read each textbook passage, and answer the questions or follow the directions provided.

A. [1]Brainstorming is thinking of as many different suggestions or ideas as possible in a short amount of time. [2]It is a useful way of thinking of creative new ideas and solutions. [3]There are four common guidelines followed by brainstorming groups. [4]First, there must be no criticism of suggestions. [5]Negative evaluations of ideas must be withheld until later. [6]The second guideline is that wild ideas are welcomed. [7]It is easier to tame down an idea than to perk it up. [8]Third, aim for quantity. [9]The greater the number of ideas, the greater the likelihood of winners. [10]The final guideline is that combinations and improvements of ideas are welcomed. [11]In addition to contributing ideas of your own, you should suggest how the ideas of others can be improved or combined.

___ 1. The main pattern of organization of the above selection is
A. list of items.
B. time order.

___ 2. Write the number of the sentence that states the main idea of the paragraph.

3. The major supporting details are introduced with the transitions *first, second, third,* and ____________________.

B. [1]Although few circumstances make us quake 'n' shake as much as speaking in public does, there are some simple ways to cope. [2]For one thing, use visual aids or handouts if possible, to take the focus off you. [3]Slides are an example of a common useful visual aid. [4]Also, have a glass of water handy. [5]This serves two purposes: It's a prop, and it helps keep the mouth moist for easy speaking. [6]Also, stand behind a desk or podium or sit at a table. [7]You'll feel and look more relaxed than if you were "free-standing." [8]Last and perhaps most important, be yourself. [9]Adopting a more formal style will make you, and your audience, less comfortable.

___ 4. The main pattern of organization of the above selection is
A. list of items.
B. time order.

5–6. Two of the transitions that signal major details of the paragraph are

____________________ and ____________________.

(Continues on next page)

C. [1]Few products last forever. [2]Most products go through distinct stages of a product life cycle. [3]The first stage in the product life cycle is the introductory stage. [4]During this first phase, the producer tries to stir up demand. [5]Typically, this stage involves expensive advertising and promotion, plus research and development costs. [6]Next comes the growth stage, marked by a rapid jump in sales as the introductory efforts start paying off. [7]As the product enters the growth phase, competition increases, and the war for market share begins. [8]During the third stage, the maturity stage, product sales begin to level off or show a slight decline. [9]The key to success in the maturity phase is to encourage sales of the existing product by broadening its appeal or making minor improvements. [10]Sooner or later most products enter the decline stage. [11]During this last phase, sales and profits begin to slip and eventually fade away.

___ 7. The main pattern of organization of the above paragraph is
A. list of items.
B. time order.

8–10. Complete the map of the paragraph by finishing the main idea heading and filling in the missing major details.

Main idea: There are distinct stages of ________________________________.

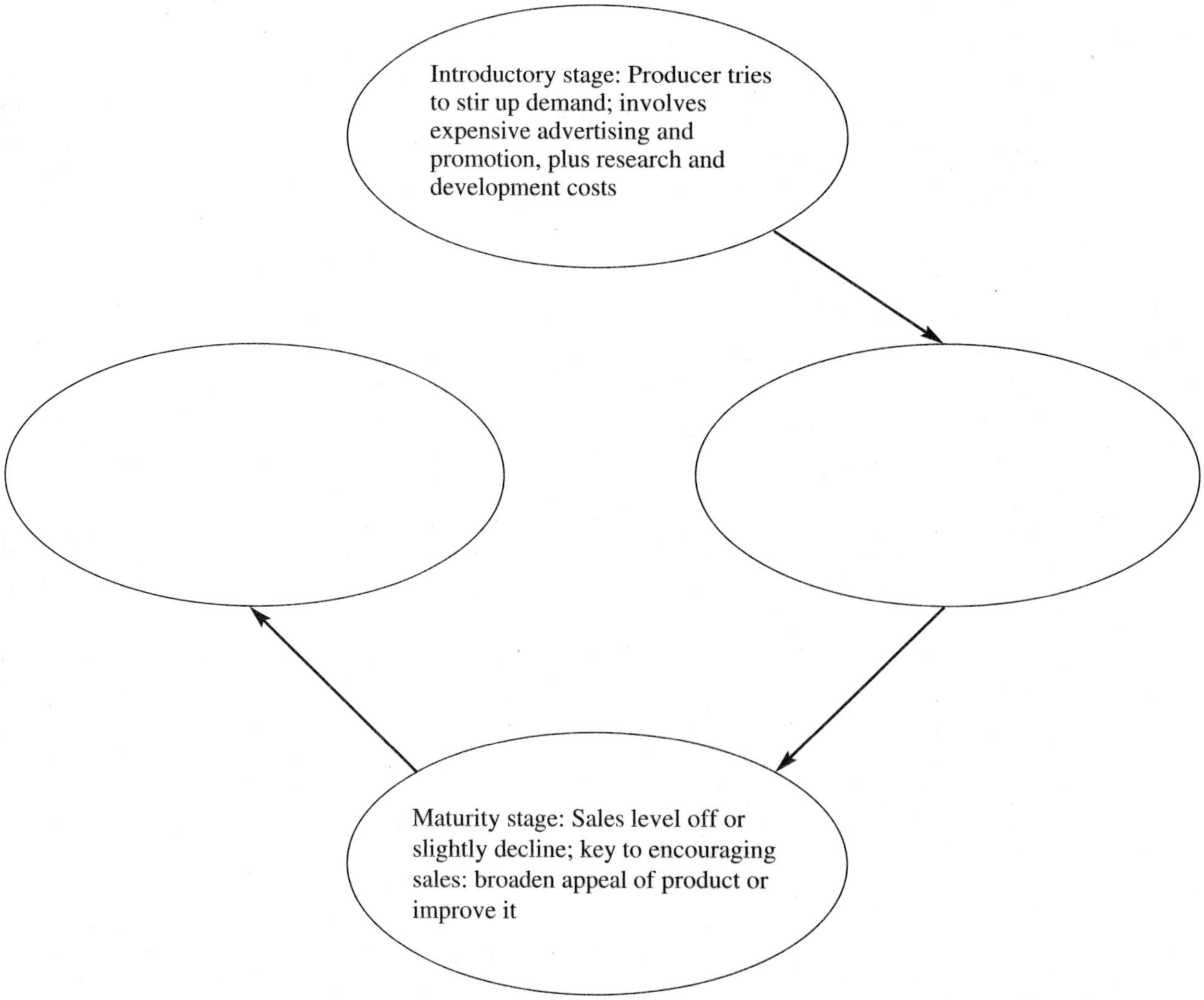
Introductory stage: Producer tries to stir up demand; involves expensive advertising and promotion, plus research and development costs
Maturity stage: Sales level off or slightly decline; key to encouraging sales: broaden appeal of product or improve it

Name ______________________

Section ____________ Date ____________

SCORE: (Number correct) × 10 = ________%

RELATIONSHIPS II: Test A

A. Fill in each blank with an appropriate transition from the box. Use each transition once. Then, in the space provided, write the letter of the transition you have chosen.

A. as a result	B. because of	C. differently
D. for example	E. in contrast	

___ 1. [1]An oldest child is treated __________________ in some ways from his or her siblings. [2]For instance, the oldest child is often given the most responsibility, including helping and teaching younger siblings.

___ 2. [1]In Russia, according to a recent study, only 50 percent of the women and 33 percent of the men said they marry for love. [2]Most said they marry because of loneliness, shared interests, or pregnancy. [3]________________, most Americans (87 percent) say they believe love is essential to a good marriage.

___ 3. [1]According to the American Cancer Society, ten to twelve million Americans regularly use chewing tobacco, including 15 percent of male high-school students and 21 percent of white males aged 18 to 24. [2]Many young men think it is cool to chew tobacco because they see professional athletes doing so. [3]However, they may not know that chewing tobacco contains grit and sand, as well as sugars to improve the taste. [4]________________, it causes tooth decay and tooth loss. [5]In addition, it can cause gum disease. [6]Finally, those who regularly chew tobacco have fifty times the risk of developing cancer than do nonusers.

___ 4. [1]Chimps and gorillas can communicate with American Sign Language. [2]By learning to make the correct signs with their hands, they can "speak" with humans and others of their species who know the signs. [3]Though the animals have vocabularies of only a few hundred signs, they respond to questions and express wishes. [4]____________________, Koko, a signing gorilla in California, asked for (and received) a kitten as a pet.

5. [1]Chocolate was grown by the Aztecs centuries before the Spanish discovered it in Mexico. [2]It reached Europe, in the form of cocoa, even before coffee and tea did. [3]It spread quickly throughout western Europe. [4]In the late nineteenth century, the Portuguese took the cocoa plant to some islands off Africa. [5]________________ the islands' ideal temperature and humidity, it became an established crop there.

(Continues on next page)

B. Label each passage with the letter of its main pattern of organization. (You may find it helpful to underline the transition or transitions in each item.)

A Definition and example
B Comparison and/or contrast
C Cause and effect

_____ 6. [1]Iced tea, cola, and other drinks that contain caffeine can actually cause you to become overheated. [2]Caffeine causes your blood vessels to become narrower, and narrower blood vessels allow less blood to flow through them. [3]And a weaker blood flow can lead to higher temperatures.

_____ 7. [1]Plea bargaining is the process by which defendants bargain away their right to a trial. [2]The defendants plead guilty to a lesser charge. [3]In return, they receive a lesser punishment than if they were found guilty of the original charge. [4]For example, a person accused of first-degree murder may plead guilty to second-degree murder.

_____ 8. [1]Today's teenagers spend billions of dollars on clothing, cosmetics, and other types of products. [2]A few reasons explain why these teens are so interested in buying things. [3]One reason is that today's teens listen to radio and watch TV many hours each week, and they are thus tempted by many advertisements. [4]Another reason is that many teens work numerous hours a week and can afford to buy themselves things.

_____ 9. [1]The Stockholm Syndrome is the name given to the way some hostages cope: by siding with the people who captured them. [2]The term comes from a 1973 Stockholm, Sweden, bank robbery in which four hostages were held captive for six days. [3]By day six, the hostages had become more loyal to the robbers than to the police. [4]One interesting example of the syndrome is a woman hostage who became attached to one of the robbers involved in her case. [5]In fact, after the incident, she broke her engagement to another man.

_____ 10. [1]In a study published in 2011, 93 obese people aged 65 and up with various physical problems were divided into four groups. [2]One group was put on a low-calorie diet and attended 90-minute exercise sessions three times a week. [3]The other three groups just dieted, just exercised, or did not change their habits. [4]After one year, the groups all took a physical performance test. [5]The dieters improved by 12 percent, and the exercisers improved by 15 percent. [6]However, the group that did both improved by 21 percent. [7]This study suggests that older people will be healthier if they combine diet and exercise than if they do just one or the other.

Name ______________________________
Section ______________ Date ___________
SCORE: (Number correct) × 10 = ________%

RELATIONSHIPS II: Test B

Read each paragraph and answer the questions that follow.

A. [1]The story of the city mouse and the country mouse is one version of the age-old debate between the people who prefer city life and those who prefer country life. [2]In the city, there is always something to do. [3]But in the country, you can always find peace and quiet. [4]In the city, you are constantly exposed to new and different kinds of people. [5]On the other hand, in the country you are always among familiar faces. [6]These are the images we have. [7]The reality is less clear-cut. [8]Rural towns do have their night spots, and New York City does have places to escape to and be alone with your thoughts.

___ 1. The main pattern of organization of the selection is
A. definition and example.
B. cause and effect.
C. comparison-contrast.

2. One transition that signals the pattern of organization is ____________________.

B. [1]A boycott is an organized refusal by people to deal with a person or group in order to reach a certain goal. [2]An example is the famous boycott that began in 1955 when Mrs. Rosa Parks of Montgomery, Alabama, refused to obey a law requiring black people to sit at the back of city buses. [3]Mrs. Parks was arrested, and her arrest sparked a boycott of the city's bus system by African Americans. [4]The boycott was organized and led by Dr. Martin Luther King, Jr. [5]Rather than continue to lose money needed to run the bus system, the city ended the law.

___ 3. The main pattern of organization of the selection is
A. definition and example.
B. comparison.
C. contrast.

4. The word that signals the pattern of organization is ________________________.

C. [1]Many people say rapid population growth is the reason why nearly one billion people go hungry every day. [2]However, political factors are also among the causes of the hunger. [3]First, many countries with hungry citizens actually export crops to other countries. [4]Exporting the crops offers greater profits than selling them at home. [5]Secondly, surpluses that could feed many people are often destroyed in order to keep the price of products high. [6]For example, some crops are allowed to rot, and extra milk is fed to pigs or even dumped.

___ 5. The main pattern of organization of the selection is
A. definition and example.
B. cause and effect.
C. comparison-contrast.

6. One word that signals the pattern of organization is ________________________.

(Continues on next page)

D. [1]The ways athletes deal with their lives after their athletic careers differ greatly. [2]When they are no longer able to perform on the court or the field, some athletes turn to drinking, taking drugs, or other destructive behaviors. [3]However, other athletes plan ahead, taking courses during their peak years and investing their money wisely. [4]For these athletes, life can be very good when the cheering of the fans stops.

___ 7. The main pattern of organization of the selection is
A. definition and example.
B. cause and effect.
C. comparison-contrast.

8. One word that signals the pattern of organization is ______________________.

E. [1]The huge earthquake that hit northern Japan on March 11, 2011 was immensely powerful. [2]In fact, its effects were felt halfway around the world. [3]The earthquake caused a massive tsunami, whose fast-moving waves washed away buildings, ships, cars, and land. [4]The waves then crossed the Pacific Ocean, ripping up docks and sinking several boats in a California harbor, and sweeping unlucky observers out to sea. [5]As a result of the earthquake and tsunami, more than ten thousand Japanese citizens died. [6]In addition, a Japanese nuclear power plant was damaged, causing dangerous radiation to be released. [7]Scientists called the quake one of the most powerful ever recorded. [8]They measured its impact as equivalent to 6.7 trillion tons of TNT—about a thousand times the power of all nuclear weapons on Earth.

___ 9. The main pattern of organization of the selection is
A. definition and example.
B. cause and effect.
C. comparison-contrast.

10. One word that signals the pattern of organization is ______________________.

Name ______________________________
Section _______________ Date ___________
SCORE: (Number correct) × 10 = ________%

RELATIONSHIPS II: Test C

Read each paragraph and answer that questions that follow.

A. [1]Some companies have found that praise can result in improvements in workers' behavior. [2]Emery Air Freight provides one such case. [3]That company announced the goal of answering all customer inquiries within ninety minutes. [4]Each customer-service representative was asked to record, on a log sheet, the time it took to answer each call. [5]If an employee's performance improved, he or she was praised by the supervisor. [6]Those who didn't improve performance were praised for their honesty and accuracy in filling out their log sheets. [7]Then they were reminded of the ninety-minute goal. [8]A few days of such feedback led to impressive results. [9]Customer-service representatives were meeting the ninety-minute deadline 90 percent of the time.

___ 1. The main idea of the paragraph is expressed in
- A. sentence 1.
- B. sentence 6.
- C. sentence 7.

___ 2. The main pattern of organization of the selection is
- A. definition and example.
- B. cause and effect.
- C. comparison-contrast.

3. One word that signals the pattern of organization is ________________________.

B. [1]Positive and negative moods affect our behavior more similarly than you might expect. [2]When we are in a good mood, we tend to be more sociable and more giving in our behavior. [3]For example, we spend more time with others, and we help others more. [4]What happens when we're in a bad mood? [5]You might think that people in a bad mood would be more withdrawn and help other people less, and sometimes this is true. [6]But often, people who are in a bad mood want to escape that mood. [7]Instead of acting in a way that is consistent with their bad mood, they try to work themselves out of it by being sociable, by helping others, or by engaging in other positive actions.

___ 4–5. *(Choose two answers.)* This selection has two patterns of organization. It
___
- A. defines and gives examples of "positive moods" and "negative moods."
- B. compares positive and negative moods.
- C. discusses the effects of positive and negative moods.

(Continues on next page)

C. [1]Language is appropriate when it is neither too formal nor too informal for the situation. [2]We need to adjust language to the specific person or group we are addressing. [3]Thus, in an interpersonal setting, we are likely to use more informal language when we are talking with our best friend and more formal language when we are talking with our grandparents. [4]In a group or public-speaking setting, we are likely to use more informal language when we are talking with our peers and more formal language when we are talking with strangers. [5]In each of these situations, the differences in our language are appropriate.

___ 6. The selection
- A. defines and illustrates formal and informal language.
- B. discusses the causes and effects of formal and informal language.
- C. contrasts the uses of formal and informal language and the settings in which they are used.

7–10. Complete the chart of the paragraph by filling in the missing details.

Kind of language	**________________ setting**	**Group or Public-Speaking setting**
____________ language	________________ ________________	When talking with our peers
Formal language	When talking with our grandparents	________________ ________________

Name ______________________

Section ____________ Date ____________

SCORE: (Number correct) × 10 = ________%

RELATIONSHIPS II: Test D

Read each paragraph and answer the questions or follow the directions provided. (You may find it helpful to mark the major and minor details as you read.)

A. [1]A common cause of fatigue is physical exhaustion. [2]Such fatigue may be caused by overdoing a difficult physical activity. [3]Waste products build up during physical activity because the body cannot remove them as quickly as they are produced. [4]These waste products cause feelings of fatigue. [5]The fatigue of physical exhaustion is also caused by using muscles that have not been used in a while. [6]Perhaps you have felt such fatigue after trying a new sport for the first time or after buffing wax on a car. [7]A second common cause of fatigue is illness. [8]Poisons from disease-causing agents get into the bloodstream and make you feel weak and tired. [9]You also have less energy when you are ill because the body uses a great deal of energy to fight the infection. [10]A third cause of fatigue is concentrating on mental tasks for a long time without taking a break. [11]Perhaps you have felt extremely tired after studying hard for a test or memorizing lines for a speech. [12]These mental tasks require a great deal of concentration and energy and can cause you to feel tired. [13]A fourth cause of fatigue is strong emotions, which can use up a great deal of mental energy. [14]For example, you might feel exhausted from having an argument with a friend. [15]Finally, boredom is another common experience that causes fatigue. [16]Your energy level can decrease and you can feel very tired just from being bored.

___ 1. The patterns of organization of the paragraph are list of items and
A. definition and example.
B. cause and effect.
C. comparison-contrast.

2–5. Complete the outline of the paragraph by finishing the implied main idea heading and filling in the missing major and minor supporting details.

Main idea: ______________________ has several causes.

1. Physical exhaustion
   a. From overdoing a difficult physical activity
   b. ______________________
2. Illness
   a. ______________________
   ____
   b. Body uses energy to fight infection
3. Concentrating on mental tasks for a long time without taking a break
4. Strong emotions
5. ______________________

(Continues on next page)

B. [1]In all but the smallest companies, more than one manager is needed to oversee the work of other employees. [2]Companies usually form a management pyramid, with more managers at the bottom than at the top and each level having its own role to play. [3]Top managers have the most power. [4]An example is the chief executive officer (CEO), who sets goals and establishes company policies. [5]Middle managers develop plans for carrying out the goals set by top management. [6]Examples are plant managers and division managers. [7]At the bottom of the pyramid are first-line managers, who oversee employees and also put into action the plans developed at higher levels. [8]Positions at this level include foreman, department head, and office manager.

___ 6. The main idea of the selection is expressed in
- A. sentence 2.
- B. sentence 3.
- C. sentence 8.

___ 7. The paragraph
- A. defines and illustrates types of managers in a typical company pyramid.
- B. contrasts types of management pyramids.
- C. explains the effects of various company organizations.

8–10. Complete the map of the paragraph by filling in the missing details.

Management Pyramid

Top managers—have the most power
(Example: Chief executive officer—sets goals and establishes policies)

______ — ______
______
______
(*Examples*: plant managers, division managers)

______ — ______
______
______
(*Examples*: ______)

Name ______________________

Section ____________ Date ____________

SCORE: (Number correct) × 10 = ________%

INFERENCES: Test A

After reading each passage, put a check by the **two** inferences that are most firmly based on the given information.

1. [1]Up through the 1700s, many Europeans believed that a king's touch could cure diseases. [2]At his coronation in 1775, for example, King Louis the Sixteenth of France touched 2,400 of his ailing subjects.

    ______ A. The touch of a king truly has special healing power others do not have.

    ______ B. There had been other kings of France named Louis.

    ______ C. French coronations were public events.

    ______ D. The French suffered more illness than other Europeans.

2. [1]Experts have blamed caffeine for bone loss among older women. [2]But a university study of 138 older women found that caffeine had no such effect. [3]In that study, women who drank more than five cups of coffee a day had the same bone density as women who got little caffeine.

    ______ A. Bone loss among older women is not a problem.

    ______ B. The experts who blamed caffeine for bone loss may be wrong.

    ______ C. Caffeine causes healthy bones.

    ______ D. Some older women have experienced bone loss.

3. [1]According to one joke, scientists are now using lawyers instead of rats in laboratory experiments. [2]There are three reasons for this change. [3]For one thing, there are more lawyers than rats. [4]For another, the scientists become less emotionally attached to the lawyers. [5]And finally, certain things are so disgusting that rats won't do them.

    ______ A. A lawyer must have made up this joke.

    ______ B. Some people feel there are too many lawyers.

    ______ C. Lawyers have the reputation of being willing to do anything.

    ______ D. Scientists have the reputation of socializing with lawyers.

(Continues on next page)

4. [1]Although lie detector tests are based on a sound principle, they are not always accurate. [2]The test is based on the fact that people become emotionally "stirred up" when they lie. [3]The lie detector can sense physical changes that accompany such emotional responses. [4]But an innocent person may react emotionally to a key question. [5]Thus, he or she appears to be lying when actually telling the truth. [6]And criminals who lie often may feel no guilt about anything. [7]They can therefore tell huge lies without showing the slightest emotional ripple on the lie detector. [8]Without an emotional response, there are no physical responses to detect.

_____ A. Criminals never feel any guilt about their crimes.

_____ B. Lie detector tests are not foolproof.

_____ C. Anyone can easily fool the lie-detector machine.

_____ D. An emotional response by an innocent person may register as a lie on a lie detector.

5. [1]Eye contact, also referred to as gaze, is how—and how much—we look at people with whom we are communicating. [2]Eye contact has several purposes in communication. [3]Its presence shows that we are paying attention. [4]In addition, how we look at a person reveals a range of emotions such as affection, anger, or fear. [5]Moreover, intensity of eye contact may also be used to show dominance. [6]For instance, we talk of someone "staring another person down." [7]Finally, through our eye contact we can check the effect of our communication. [8]By maintaining our eye contact, we can tell when or whether people are paying attention to us, when people are involved in what we are saying, and what their feelings are about what we are saying.

_____ A. Eye contact can be a clue to what we feel and what our listeners feel.

_____ B. Our eyes are more important than our ears in effective communication..

_____ C. Eye contact can never reveal how much power one person has over another.

_____ D. Sometimes a parent can control children just by looking at them.

Name ______________________________

Section ______________ Date ___________

SCORE: (Number correct) × 10 = ________%

INFERENCES: Test B

A. After reading the passage, put a check by the **two** inferences that are most firmly based on the given information.

1. [1]Two groups of students were gathered as "jurors" in an imaginary court case. [2]One group was told that the defendant was named Carlos Ramirez and that he was from Albuquerque, New Mexico. [3]The other group learned that the defendant was Robert Johnson from Dayton, Ohio. [4]Both groups heard the same evidence against the defendant. [5]When it was time to decide a verdict, the majority of "jurors" found that Ramirez was guilty and that Johnson was innocent.

_____ A. The "court case" was actually an experiment about racial prejudice.

_____ B. The students were Hispanic.

_____ C. The evidence was based upon an actual court case.

_____ D. The experiment revealed the existence of negative stereotypes about Hispanics.

2. [1]The manufacture and sale of alcoholic beverages was outlawed in 1919 by the Eighteenth Amendment. [2]Prohibition, as it was called, achieved a number of good results. [3]It lowered the average consumption of alcohol. [4]Arrests for drunkenness fell sharply. [5]The rate of alcoholism was reduced. [6]If the Prohibitionists had been willing to legalize beer and wine, the experiment might have worked. [7]Instead, by insisting on a totally "dry" society, they drove thousands of ordinary people to break the law.

_____ A. During Prohibition, alcohol was not available.

_____ B. During Prohibition, many usually law-abiding people drank illegally.

_____ C. The Prohibitionists opposed the use of any form of alcoholic beverage.

_____ D. The Prohibitionists were tolerant of moderate social drinking.

(Continues on next page)

B. After reading each short passage, put a check by the **three** inferences that are most firmly based on the given information.

3. [1]Your sister has a new boyfriend. [2]The first time you meet him, he corners you and talks to you for an hour about football, a subject in which you have no interest at all. [3]You come away with the impression that he is an inconsiderate bore. [4]The next two times you see him, however, he says not a word about football. [5]He participates in the general conversation and makes some witty and intelligent remarks. [6]What is your impression of him now? [7]Do you find him likable and interesting on the basis of the last two encounters? [8]Do you average out the early minus and the later plus and come out with a neutral zero? [9]Neither is likely. [10]What is likely is that you still think of him as an inconsiderate bore. [11]Psychological research suggests that first impressions, as our mothers and fathers told us, are quite lasting.

_____ A. The words "neutral zero" refer to an impression that is positive.

_____ B. The words "neutral zero" refer to an impression that is neither positive nor negative.

_____ C. The selection suggests that it's a good idea to make good first impressions.

_____ D. The selection suggests that it can be difficult to remain objective about others.

_____ E. First impressions tend to be fair and balanced impressions.

4. [1]Sociologists distinguish between primary and secondary groups. [2]A primary group is two or more people who enjoy a direct, intimate relationship with one another. [3]We emotionally commit ourselves to a primary group. [4]We view its members—friends, family members, and lovers—as worthwhile and important. [5]They are not simply a means to other ends. [6]A secondary group consists of two or more people who have come together for a specific, practical purpose. [7]The relationship is a means to an end, not an end in itself. [8]Illustrations include our relationships with a clerk in a clothing store and a cashier at a service station.

_____ A. Our secondary groups change more frequently than our primary groups do.

_____ B. It is more difficult to replace a member of a secondary group than a member of a primary group.

_____ C. A favorite teacher is likely to be a member of a student's primary group.

_____ D. It would be difficult to function in society without the aid of secondary group members.

_____ E. Members of our primary group have more power over us emotionally than members of our secondary groups.

Name ______________________________
Section ______________ Date ____________
SCORE: (Number correct) × 10 = ________%

INFERENCES: Test C

A. (1–2.) After reading the short passage, put a check by the **two** inferences that are most firmly based on the given information.

[1]Experimenters showed young children one of two short films. [2]In film "A," an adult was shown attacking an inflatable doll. [3]She sat on the toy, punched it in the nose, and threw it about the room. [4]In film "B," the same adult was shown playing quietly with the doll. [5]Later, the children were allowed to play in a room containing many toys, including the inflatable doll. [6]The children who had seen film "A" were much more likely to attack the doll than the children who had seen film "B."

_____ 1. The experiment proved that children are more violent than adults.

_____ 2. The experiment probably was designed to find out if children are influenced by the violence they see.

_____ 3. The results of the experiment suggest that one way children learn to be violent is by seeing violence.

_____ 4. The children who saw film "A" were more violent to begin with.

B. (3–5.) After reading the short passage, put a check by the **three** inferences that are most firmly based on the given information.

[1]Hobbies can serve as promising springboards for business ventures. [2]But to succeed in business, you must balance your creative skills with a knowledge of business techniques. [3]Hobbyists can get the business experience they need in two ways. [4]First, go to work for someone else before going into business for yourself. [5]Consider this first step an apprenticeship in the sort of venture you want to start. [6]Soak up all you can about the problems, the opportunities, and the necessary technical skills. [7]Or you can go directly into business if you have a partner strong in management experience. [8]A hobbyist chef and an experienced restaurant manager may have the right combination of skills to get a venture off the ground.

_____ 1. Being a fine cook is not a good enough qualification for opening a restaurant.

_____ 2. The restaurant business is one of the riskiest ones for a hobbyist to enter.

_____ 3. Creative skills are more important to a business's success than business experience.

_____ 4. Building a successful business requires background in the company's product or service and in business techniques.

_____ 5. A hobbyist chef can get important business experience by working at someone else's restaurant.

(Continues on next page)

C. (6–10.) Read the following textbook passage. Then check the **five** statements which are most logically supported by the information given.

[1]Research has suggested that people are often overly influenced by immediate rewards. [2]Consider a student who has an early morning class in a course in which it is important to attend each lecture. [3]The night before a class, the student decides that a good grade in the course (a delayed reward) is more important than an hour of extra sleep. [4]So he sets his alarm in time to attend the lecture. [5]When the alarm rings the next morning, however, the student changes his mind. [6]Now he chooses extra sleep over a good grade. [7]The immediate reward, extra sleep, now has greater control over his behavior than the delayed reward, a good grade. [8]The power of immediate rewards can be seen in many other situations. [9]Examples are when a person on a diet is confronted with a piece of chocolate cake or when someone trying to save money sees an attractive item in a store window.

[10]Psychologists have developed techniques that dieters, impulsive spenders, and those who tend to oversleep can use when trying to avoid the power of immediate rewards. [11]For example, a student with an early morning class can ask a classmate to stop by on the way to class. [12]That would make it awkward and embarrassing to stay in bed. [13]An impulsive spender may be advised to carry no credit cards and very little cash, making it more difficult to go on a spending spree.

_____ 1. The student who oversleeps generally feels good about his decision to miss class.

_____ 2. Although immediate rewards can be pleasurable, they often interfere with our delayed rewards.

_____ 3. The closer a reward is, the less tempting it becomes.

_____ 4. Since delayed rewards are so hard to achieve, people should avoid them.

_____ 5. To someone trying to quit smoking, a cigarette would be a delayed reward.

_____ 6. To someone on a diet, losing several pounds would be a delayed reward.

_____ 7. Immediate rewards can be more tempting than delayed rewards that are much more important.

_____ 8. Delayed rewards are easier to get than immediate rewards.

_____ 9. Delayed rewards are often of greater long-term value than immediate rewards.

_____ 10. To achieve delayed rewards, it can help to find ways to avoid the temptations of immediate rewards.

Name ______________________________

Section ______________ Date ____________

SCORE: (Number correct) × 10 = ________%

INFERENCES: Test D

A. (1–5.) Read the following textbook passage. Then check the **five** statements which are most logically supported by the information given.

[1]What would you do if you won ten million dollars in a lottery? [2]Your first reaction might be, "I'd spend the rest of my life on the beach (or skiing or traveling)." [3]But in all likelihood you, like most other people who receive financial windfalls, would seek some kind of work eventually. [4]A variety of motives keeps people working, even when they don't need a paycheck to survive. [5]If you've ever worked as a volunteer, you know that helping someone can be more satisfying than receiving pay. [6]Work also provides a sense of identity. [7]One man aged 81 said, "I've been in the fabric business since I was a kid, and I still get a kick out of it."

[8]Studies suggest that rats, pigeons, and children sometimes work to gain rewards, even if they can get the same rewards without working. [9]One researcher wrote the following on the subject:

> [10]Rats will run down an alley tripping over hundreds of food pellets to obtain a single, identical pellet in the goal box, . . . and pigeons will peck a key . . . to get exactly the same food that is freely available in a nearby cup. [11]Given the choice of receiving marbles merely by waiting a certain amount of time for their delivery, children tend to prefer to press a lever . . . to get the same marbles.

_____ 1. Serving a purpose is satisfying.

_____ 2. It is not so lucky to win a large amount of money in a lottery.

_____ 3. Endless "vacationing" eventually becomes dissatisfying.

_____ 4. The pay we receive is unimportant.

_____ 5. Most people try to work as little as possible.

_____ 6. People, rats, and pigeons enjoy the challenges and interaction that work offers.

_____ 7. It generally feels better to achieve something than to be given something.

_____ 8. People who don't retire continue to work only because they need the money.

_____ 9. Most people who work as volunteers resent the fact that they are not paid for their work.

_____ 10. Work can be its own reward.

(Continues on next page)

B. (6–10.) Read the following textbook passage. Then check the **five** statements which are most logically supported by the information given.

[1]In the late nineteenth century, proper heterosexual courtship took the form of "calling." [2]When a young woman reached marriageable age, she was allowed to receive male callers in her home, under the watchful eye of a chaperone. [3]The entire calling system was controlled by women and took place in their sphere. [4]A young man was allowed to pay a call only if he was definitely invited by a young woman or her mother. [5]It was considered highly unsuitable for a man to force his attention on a lady by making the first move.

[6]By the mid-1920s, an entirely new system of courtship—the date—had taken over. [7]Couples who dated no longer sat together in the front parlor of a private home. [8]They went out to theaters, restaurants, and dance halls. [9]This move into the public sphere gave couples unheard-of freedom. [10]It also changed power relations between the sexes. [11]Men, who controlled the public sphere, now controlled courtship. [12]Now women were forbidden to take the first step. [13]According to mid-twentieth-century advice manuals, girls who refused to respect "the time-honored custom of waiting for boys to take the first step" would ruin a good dating career.

_____ 1. Mothers would definitely have preferred the dating system to the calling system.

_____ 2. Under the system of calling, women saw only those men in whom they or their mothers were genuinely interested.

_____ 3. A nineteenth-century man who showed up uninvited at a woman's home would be considered ill-mannered.

_____ 4. What is considered proper in one generation may be improper in another.

_____ 5. Despite the differences in customs, the same rules of proper behavior continue from generation to generation.

_____ 6. Chaperones were still common in the 1920s.

_____ 7. Parents had less control over dating than they had over calling.

_____ 8. Changes in the rules for courtship take many generations.

_____ 9. It would have been easier for young couples to have sexual relations in the late nineteenth century than in the mid-1920s.

_____ 10. In the late nineteenth century, it could have been difficult for a young man and young woman to be alone.

Name ______________________

Section __________ Date __________

SCORE: (Number correct) × 10 = ______%

IMPLIED MAIN IDEAS: Test A

A. In the space provided, write the letter of the general idea that best covers the specific ideas. Remember that the correct general idea will not be too narrow or too broad. It will describe what the specific ideas have in common.

___ 1. *Specific ideas:* horror, shame, disgust, fear

The general idea is
A. emotions.
B. calm emotions.
C. unpleasant emotions.

___ 2. *Specific ideas:* infant, toddler, grade schooler, teenager

The general idea is
A. stages.
B. stages of life.
C. stages of youth.

___ 3. *Specific ideas:* lose weight, quit smoking, cut down on fats, eat more fiber

The general idea is
A. ways to cure illness.
B. ways to become healthier.
C. ways to become richer.

___ 4. *Specific ideas:* mascara, night cream, hair spray, lipstick

The general idea is
A. beauty products.
B. makeup.
C. items bought in a drugstore.

___ 5. *Specific ideas:* California, New York, Georgia, Rhode Island

The general idea is
A. states.
B. large states.
C. northern states.

___ 6. *Specific ideas:* "Ouch, that hurts," "Oh, my aching back," "The children upstairs are too noisy," "My teacher assigns too much work"

The general idea is:
A. complaints.
B. comments.
C. complaints about physical pain.

(Continues on next page)

___ 7. *Specific ideas:* staples, Scotch tape, pens, paper clips

The general idea is

A. office supplies.

B. items for fastening papers.

C. office items that are sharp.

___ 8. *Specific ideas:* "See you," "Bye," "Catch you later," "So long"

The general idea is

A. words used in conversations.

B. words used to say good-bye.

C. words.

B. (9–10.) Each group is made up of four sentences with an unstated main idea. Write the letter of the answer that best states the implied main idea of each group.

Group 1

1. Many college students budget their time poorly and thus often feel anxious about unfinished tasks.
2. Students may feel so much pressure to do well that they work constantly, allowing little time for rest or recreation.
3. Cramped and crowded dormitories can be noisy and unpleasant.
4. Students may feel great pressure to act in certain ways in order to be accepted by a particular group.

___ The unstated main idea of these sentences is:

A. It is important for students to allow sufficient time for rest and relaxation.

B. College can be a very stressful experience.

C. Some college students care more about social acceptance than their own standards.

D. Learning to budget one's time is an essential part of succeeding in college.

Group 2

1. In 1833, Oberlin College became the nation's first coeducational college.
2. In 1837, Mary Lyon established the first women's college, Mount Holyoke, to train teachers and missionaries.
3. Three colleges for blacks were founded before the Civil War.
4. A few other colleges—including Oberlin, Harvard and Dartmouth—admitted small numbers of black students in the nineteenth century.

___ The unstated main idea of these sentences is:

A. In a democracy, a college education should be available to members of all groups.

B. Women could first go to college in the United States in the 1800s.

C. It was in the 1800s that women and African-Americans were first able to go to college in the United States.

D. Several of the nation's colleges are well over 150 years old.

Name ______________________
Section ____________ Date ____________
SCORE: (Number correct) × 10 = ________%

IMPLIED MAIN IDEAS: Test B

A. In the following items, the specific ideas are given, but the general ideas are unstated. Fill in the blanks with the unstated general ideas.

1. *General idea:* ______________________________
   Specific ideas: poached, scrambled, sunny-side up, fried

2. *General idea:* ______________________________
   Specific ideas: linoleum, carpeting, rugs, ceramic tile

3. *General idea:* ______________________________
   Specific ideas: organize coupons, look through cupboards, make a list, check supermarket ads

4. *General idea:* ______________________________
   Specific ideas: fireplace, wood stove, oil burner, heat pump

5. *General idea:* ______________________________
   Specific ideas: do research, write rough draft, prepare outline, type final copy

6. *General idea:* ______________________________
   Specific ideas: Amen, The End, And they lived happily ever after., That's all, folks!

7. *General idea:* ______________________________
   Specific ideas: zebra, tiger, candy cane, barbershop pole

8. *General idea:* ______________________________
   Specific ideas: snakes, flying in an airplane, heights, being in small spaces

(Continues on next page)

B. Write the letter of the implied main idea of each of the following two paragraphs.

___ 9. [1]One clue to what a textbook chapter is about is its title. [2]Also, the chapter may begin with a short overview—a paragraph or a list of points with a heading such as "Chapter Preview" or "Learning Objectives." [3]Opening material like this is your second clue. [4]It lets you know what major topics will be covered. [5]For a third type of clue, look at the headings and subheadings within the chapter, to see how the subject matter is organized. [6]They tell you about relationships among the topics. [7]Other helpful clues are visual aids: tables, charts, graphs, and photos. [8]These are usually included to highlight important material. [9]For further clues, look for key words emphasized in boldface or color. [10]These are vocabulary terms you will need to know.

A. A textbook chapter contains several elements.
B. You can learn what a textbook chapter is about by looking at several clues.
C. Some parts of a textbook chapter are more important than others.
D. Key words are often emphasized by the use of boldface or color.

___10. [1]In the ancient kingdom of Babylonia, a man named Enlil-Bani was chosen to be "king for a day" as part of the New Year's celebration. [2]Enlil-Bani was the real king's gardener. [3]According to custom, the mock king would rule for a day and then would be killed as a sacrifice to the gods. [4]In Enlil-Bani's case, however, the real king died during the celebration. [5]As a result, the lucky gardener remained on the throne for twenty-four years.

A. Ancient civilizations were extremely brutal.
B. Babylonians believed in human sacrifices.
C. A doomed Babylonian gardener became a king by accident.
D. The Babylonians had a deadly New Year's custom that ended in human sacrifice.

Name ______________________

Section ____________ Date ____________

SCORE: (Number correct) × 20 = ________%

IMPLIED MAIN IDEAS: Test C

Write the letter of the implied main idea in each of the following paragraphs.

___ 1. [1]In his book *Anatomy of an Illness,* writer Norman Cousins described his battle with a severe joint ailment. [2]Told that his doctors could do no more for him, he checked out of the hospital and into a pleasant hotel room. [3]He spent weeks watching Marx Brothers movies and other comedies. [4]He read the funniest authors he could find. He joked and wisecracked with his visitors. [5]Cousins' health improved so much that his doctors were amazed.

A. Doctors could not do anything to cure Cousins' joint problem.
B. The Marx Brothers were the stars of movie comedies.
C. Norman Cousins had a severe joint ailment.
D. Cousins' experience suggests that laughter may help to heal the body.

___ 2. [1]We're often told "He who hesitates is lost," but we're also warned to "look before you leap." [2]Most of us have heard the saying, "Out of sight, out of mind," but then we hear "Absence makes the heart grow fonder." [3]Everyone talks about "love at first sight." [4]But then someone reminds us, "Marry in haste, repent at leisure." [5]It's all very confusing.

A. "He who hesitates is lost" seems to be the opposite of "Look before you leap."
B. Absence does not make the heart grow fonder.
C. "Love at first sight" is a myth.
D. Some common sayings seem to contradict each other.

___ 3. [1]Rock, which was first called rock and roll, includes several different styles. [2]All of those styles, however, focus on vocal music—one or more singers—often accompanied by electric guitars. [3]Other common rock instruments are electric instruments, including the bass and drums. [4]All forms of rock feature a hard, pounding, very powerful beat. [5]Another feature is loudness, often so great it can damage players' hearing.

A. Rock is played by certain characteristic instruments.
B. The various styles of rock have totally different features.
C. All styles of rock share certain distinct features.
D. Electronic instruments help to make rock loud.

(Continues on next page)

___ 4. [1]At nine months many infants are watching television, though not necessarily understanding it. [2]By three or four years of age, they average four hours of TV a day. [3]In middle childhood and adolescence, twenty to twenty-five hours a week is about average. [4]Some youngsters manage a forty-hour week in front of the tube.

A. Children start to watch television when they are very young.
B. As children get older, they watch more and more television.
C. Some children watch television for as much as forty hours a week.
D. Too much television is bad for children.

___ 5. [1]Nearly all people at times feel sad and think things are hopeless. [2]Depressed by some event or circumstance, they may be unable to perform their normal activities. [3]Also, they may have no appetite. [4]This type of depression affects nearly everyone; as a result, psychiatrists often refer to it as "the common cold of mental illness." [5]However, for some individuals, depression is a more extreme condition. [6]This state, called clinical depression, is more lasting and seems to be unrelated to any stressful life event.

A. There are two types of depression.
B. Most people feel depressed at times.
C. Depression is like the common cold.
D. Clinical depression is a serious illness.

Name ______________________________
Section ______________ Date ____________
SCORE: (Number correct) × 20 = ________%

IMPLIED MAIN IDEAS: Test D

Write the letter of the implied main idea in each of the following paragraphs.

___ 1. [1]The first step in answering a multiple-choice item is to read it carefully. [2]This will help you see exactly what you are being asked, so that you don't answer the wrong question—an all-too-common mistake. [3]Second, think how you would answer the item if *no* choices were given. [4]If your own answer matches one of the choices, that may be the right one. [5]Third, look at all the choices. [6]No matter how sure you may feel, your first reaction might be wrong, so it's a smart idea to consider each option. [7]Fourth, if you don't know the answer, make an "educated guess" by eliminating any choices that are obviously wrong. [8]This improves your chance of picking the right choice.

A. Read a multiple-choice question carefully before you answer it.
B. There are four steps to follow when you answer multiple-choice questions.
C. It's all right to guess when you answer multiple-choice questions.
D. Multiple-choice questions are the most common form of test questions.

___ 2. [1]If you have an automobile accident, stop immediately, but try not to block traffic. [2]Keep calm. [3]Be polite—don't blame or accuse the other driver. [4]Help anyone who has been injured, but don't try to move someone who is seriously hurt. [5]Call the police at once. [6]When they arrive, answer their questions calmly. [7]Get, and write down for yourself, the following information about each car and driver involved: name, address, license plate number, make and model of car, insurance company. [8]Notify your own insurance company as soon as possible, usually within twenty-four hours.

A. Automobile accidents happen to everyone.
B. Because accidents happen, you should definitely have automobile insurance.
C. Here's what you should do if you are involved in an automobile accident.
D. If you're involved in an automobile accident, call the police immediately.

___ 3. [1]One frequent sleep problem among children is known as "night terrors." [2]A child suffering from night terrors will wake up screaming and frightened, but without a memory of any scary dream. [3]Another common sleep disturbance, of course, is the nightmare. [4]Most children occasionally suffer from frightening dreams that make them wake up terrified. [5]Sleepwalking and talking during sleep are other common childhood problems that interfere with sleep. [6]Also, some children develop nighttime fears that make getting to sleep difficult, such as the belief that there is a monster hiding under their bed.

A. "Night terrors" are a frequent sleep problem among children.
B. Children's sleep problems can be prevented.
C. Nightmares are the most common form of sleep disturbance.
D. There are several common sleep problems in childhood.

(Continues on next page)

___ 4. [1]The death of a loved one, especially a husband or wife, is usually ranked as the most stressful event a person can experience. [2]Other experiences that cause great stress are a life-threatening illness and a serious accident or injury. [3]Divorce, loss of a job, and being a victim of crime are also very stressful. [4]But positive events can cause stress too. [5]Examples are a new job (even if it's a better one), marriage, a new baby, and even a vacation trip.

A. The worst thing that can happen to a person is the death of a loved one.
B. Serious injuries and life-threatening illnesses are major sources of stress.
C. Stress can be caused by both positive and negative experiences.
D. Stress is a normal part of everyone's life.

___ 5. [1]Every ten seconds a home or business somewhere in the United States is broken into, according to police reports. [2]Many houses broken into are unlocked, so the first and most logical protection is to keep doors and windows locked. [3]Another way to protect against burglaries is to have a security system linked to an alarm company that will call the police if a break-in occurs. [4]But the most effective preventive of all against break-ins, according to career criminals, is a large dog.

A. There are three good ways to protect against burglaries.
B. The number of burglaries in the United States is increasing.
C. Locking doors and windows will protect a house from burglary.
D. Most criminals are afraid of large dogs.

Name ______________________

Section ____________ Date __________

SCORE: (Number correct) × 10 = ________%

THE BASICS OF ARGUMENT: Test A

A. In each of the following groups, one statement is the point, and the other statements are support for the point. Identify each point with a **P** and each statement of support with an **S**.

Group 1

_____ 1. Ravi arrived at work a half hour late because of a huge traffic jam.

_____ 2. A pen leaked ink on Ravi's new shirt just before he had to go to a meeting with his boss.

_____ 3. Ravi slipped and fell in the middle of the hallway in front of all his coworkers.

_____ 4. Ravi is having a bad day.

Group 2

_____ 5. Millions of bacteria live and breed on human skin.

_____ 6. Tiny mites live in people's hair and on their beds, feeding on dead skin.

_____ 7. The human body is home to many different creatures.

_____ 8. Microscopic worm-like creatures live in the eyelashes of most people, enjoying the warmth and safety of the human eye.

B. (9.) Below is a point followed by three clusters of information. Put a check (✓) next to the **one** cluster that logically supports the point.

Point: This past winter was very severe.

_____ A. [1]The East got its usual amount of snow, and cold air swept over areas from the Midwest to the West Coast. [2]In Minnesota, temperatures were below zero for two weeks, as is usually the case. [3]The South was a bit chilly, but nothing out of the ordinary.

_____ B. [1]In January, heavy snows blanketed most of the country, even areas that rarely see snow. [2]At the end of December, severe flooding caused millions of dollars of damage in several coastal states. [3]Several huge ice storms knocked power out for millions of people this winter. [4]Most agree this was the worst winter in recent memory.

_____ C. [1]Some areas of the Midwest normally have temperatures below zero. [2]However, most of this winter was warm enough for people to wear light jackets. [3]In the Northeast, there was very little snow. [4]And in the South, trees and flowers started their spring growth early because the ground was so warm.

(Continues on next page)

C. (10.) Read the three items of supporting evidence below. Then write the letter of the point that is most logically supported by that evidence.

Support:

- The new mall—with two department stores, various specialty stores, and restaurants—provides one-stop shopping.
- The new mall has plenty of indoor and outdoor parking.
- Many local seniors like to walk in the new mall because it's safe and air-conditioned.

____ **Point:** Which of the following conclusions is best supported by all the evidence above?

A. Every town needs a mall.
B. The new mall is pleasant and convenient.
C. Malls are important to the nation's economy.
D. The new mall will find it difficult to compete with a large discount store nearby.

Name ______________________
Section ____________ Date ____________
SCORE: (Number correct) × 10 = ________%

THE BASICS OF ARGUMENT: Test B

A. Each point is followed by three statements that provide logical support and two that do not. In the spaces, write the letters of the **three** logical statements of support.

Point: My next-door neighbors are inconsiderate.

A. They let their dogs wander around in my yard whenever I am not home.
B. They pile their garbage next to my fence so that the smell blows into my kitchen window.
C. The man drives his daughter to school each morning just as I am waking up.
D. They play loud music in the middle of the night—even on a work night.
E. He and his wife like to plant flowers in their front yard.

1–3. *Items that logically support the point:* _____ _____ _____

Point: Building a house on beachfront property is a bad idea.

A. Beachfront properties provide beautiful views for homeowners.
B. One out of three beachfront homes is damaged or destroyed by storms.
C. It is very difficult to get insurance for the special problems of beachfront homes.
D. Ocean levels are expected to rise over the next few years, causing even more damage to beachfront properties.
E. Some of the most expensive houses in the country are on beachfront land.

4–6. *Items that logically support the point:* _____ _____ _____

Point: A curfew of 9 p.m. should be set for all teenagers.

A. Teenage drivers cause 75 percent of all accidents that happen after 9 p.m.
B. Not all teenagers are troublemakers.
C. Most crimes involving teenagers happen in the evenings.
D. Many teens have to work at their jobs after 9 p.m.
E. On average, teenagers who are home during the evenings have higher grades than those who are not.

7–9. *Items that logically support the point:* _____ _____ _____

(Continues on next page)

B. (10.) Below is a point followed by three clusters of information. Put a check next to the **one** cluster that logically supports the point.

Point: Ralph has serious financial problems.

_____ A. [1]He bought a new car this year even though his last car was only three years old. [2]He recently took his girlfriend on an expensive trip to Hawaii. [3]They stayed at a nice hotel and ate all their meals out. [4]While they were there, he proposed marriage to her and gave her an expensive diamond ring he had just bought.

_____ B. [1]All of his credit cards have high balances; one of his accounts has been sent to a collection agency. [2]His rent payment almost equals his monthly salary. [3]And he still owes thousands of dollars in student loans.

_____ C. [1]He has asthma, which makes him cough and wheeze almost daily. [2]In addition, he has bad knees from an old football injury. [3]Last year, his knees became so sore that he stopped exercising and started to gain weight. [4]Today he is so overweight that his doctor is worried about him.

Name ______________________

Section ____________ Date ____________

SCORE: (Number correct) × 10 = ________%

THE BASICS OF ARGUMENT: Test C

A. In the following group, one statement is the point, and the other statements are support for the point. Identify the point with a **P** and each statement of support with an **S**.

_____ 1. People who have pets tend to resist diseases better than others.

_____ 2. Studies show that people who own dogs and cats have a lower risk of heart disease.

_____ 3. Pet ownership is healthy for people.

_____ 4. Petting an animal can lower blood pressure by as much as 15 percent.

B. Each point below is followed by three clusters of information. Put a check (✓) next to the **one** cluster that logically supports the point.

5. **Point:** Lena is courteous and kind.

_____ A. [1]Wherever she goes, she asks a lot of questions. [2]She always wants to know what is going on. [3]She reads newspapers, magazines, and books because she wants to learn. [4]In her college classes, her teachers always spend a portion of their class time answering her questions.

_____ B. [1]Whenever she goes to the store, she volunteers to help older people who are loading their cars. [2]If she drives past someone whose car has broken down, she stops and offers to help. [3]And when it snows, she shovels her elderly neighbor's driveway before she does her own.

_____ C. [1]She talks to everyone. [2]If she goes to the supermarket, she ends up getting into a discussion with the cashier or another customer waiting in line. [3]Even though she just moved last month, she already knows many people on her block because she talks to them as they walk by her apartment.

6. **Point:** The house on the corner has a long, interesting history.

_____ A. [1]The paint on the house is faded and flaking off. [2]One of the windows in the attic is missing, and the shingles on the roof are worn and curled. [3]There are small cracks in several of the house's walls, and the curtains in the windows are yellow and torn.

_____ B. [1]Neighbors report hearing noises coming from the house late at night, but no one lives there. [2]An odd black cat sometimes sits on the front step of the house but runs away before anyone can pet it. [3]A few kids said they once saw strange green and blue lights flickering in the second-floor bedroom.

_____ C. [1]The house was built long before the roads were paved. [2]Over a hundred years ago it was used as a post office. [3]Later it became a small general store, selling goods to those who came to pan for gold. [4]Only in the last fifty years was it devoted entirely to being just a house.

(Continues on next page)

C. The point below is followed by three statements that provide logical support and two that do not. In the spaces, write the letters of the **three** logical statements of support.

Point: Being a volunteer can be a very positive experience.

A. Finding time to do volunteer work is difficult, especially for parents of young children.
B. Volunteer work helps people get to know each other better.
C. Doing volunteer work teaches people about the difficulties that others face.
D. By volunteering, many people learn skills that they can use in their jobs.
E. Some volunteer work can only be done by people with special skills.

7–9. *Items that logically support the point:* _____ _____ _____

D. (10.) Read the three items of supporting evidence below. Then write the letter of the point that is most logically supported by that evidence.

Support:

- Many small movie theaters have closed because they could not compete with the large new multiplexes with many screens.
- Small corner bookshops have lost the battle with huge new bookstores.
- Neighborhood hardware stores have been forced out of business by giant "home and garden" warehouse centers.

___ **Point:** Which of the following conclusions is best supported by all the evidence above?

A. People enjoy the personal connection at small, local stores.
B. Bigger bookstores have more books to offer than small bookstores.
C. In recent years, very large businesses have forced many small ones to close.
D. Some small theaters have managed to stay open by charging very low prices for tickets.

Name ________________________________

Section _______________ Date ___________

SCORE: (Number correct) × 10 = ________%

THE BASICS OF ARGUMENT: Test D

A. In the following group, one statement is the point, and the other statements are support for the point. Identify the point with a **P** and each statement of support with an **S**.

_____ 1. Undercooked meat may contain worms and parasites that can infect people.

_____ 2. Healthy food preparation requires care in cleaning and cooking.

_____ 3. Unwashed fruits and vegetables are usually coated in chemicals that can be harmful to the body.

_____ 4. Dishes and counters that aren't cleaned properly can spread disease-carrying bacteria.

B. Below is a point followed by three clusters of information. Put a check (✓) next to the **one** cluster that logically supports the point.

5. **Point:** Suburban growth has caused environmental problems throughout the nation.

_____ A. [1]The growth of suburbs has threatened the water supply of several cities, including Phoenix and Las Vegas. [2]In the Northeast, suburban sprawl has greatly reduced the land available for wildlife. [3]And new suburbs in the Midwest have brought air pollution to areas that were once prairies.

_____ B. [1]New housing construction in suburbs provides jobs. [2]It also raises tax dollars and increases property value. [3]In addition, new housing leads to economic growth by creating the need for other kinds of businesses—stores, hospitals, schools, banks, etc.

_____ C. [1]Suburban growth lures jobs and people out of cities. [2]In the Northeast, so many people and businesses have moved to suburbs that the cities have begun to decay. [3]Across the nation, fewer people are left to pay city taxes. [4]As a result, city services often don't have enough money to operate properly.

C. The point below is followed by three statements that provide logical support and two that do not. In the spaces, write the letters of the **three** logical statements of support.

Point: Junk mail should be outlawed.

A. Many companies make millions of dollars worth of sales through their use of junk mail.
B. Each year millions of tons of paper are wasted on junk mail nobody wants.
C. The manufacturing of the ink and paper used to make junk mail contributes to the nation's pollution problems.
D. Some people don't mind receiving junk mail; some even enjoy it.
E. Too much of our precious landfill space is used up by junk mail that is thrown away.

6–8. *Items that logically support the point:* _____ _____ _____

(Continues on next page)

D. (9–10.) For each group, read the three items of supporting evidence. Then write the letter of the point that is most logically supported by that evidence.

Group 1

Support:

- The birthrate for women aged 40–44 more than doubled over the last thirty years.
- Between 1970 and 2006, the percentage of women who had a first child after age 35 increased 800 percent.
- Since 1970, the birthrate of women in their twenties has declined.

___ **Point:** Which of the following conclusions is best supported by all the evidence above?

A. Women are having fewer babies today than they used to.
B. Women shouldn't wait so long to have their babies.
C. Women today are having their children later in life than they used to.
D. Teenagers are having fewer and fewer babies each year.

Group 2

Support:

- Attractive displays are placed at the ends of aisles to get people to buy the products.
- Necessities such as milk and bread are kept deep in the store so customers must pass many other aisles to get to them—perhaps buying other things along the way.
- Impulse items, such as candy and magazines, are placed near supermarket check-out lines so people will buy them just before they leave the store.

___ **Point:** Which of the following conclusions is best supported by all the evidence above?

A. By buying impulse items, people can spend much more than they intended to.
B. Supermarkets want to help customers use good spending and eating habits.
C. Supermarkets use special methods to get people to spend more money.
D. Most of the products sold by supermarkets are overpriced and unhealthy.

Name ______________________________

Section ______________ Date ___________

SCORE: (Number correct) × 12.5 = _______%

COMBINED SKILLS: Test A

After reading the passage, write the letter of the best answer to each question.

[1]The effect of sleep deprivation on your test-taking ability depends on the type of exam questions. [2]If they're multiple choice or true/false questions, a night without sleep won't affect your ability to deal with them. [3]The reason is that in answering such questions you rely on familiar, established problem-solving techniques. [4]Such techniques are unaffected by the loss of one night's sleep. [5]If, however, your exam included essay questions, you'd be in trouble. [6]To answer this type of question, you need to think flexibly. [7]And this ability is diminished after only a single sleepless night.

___ 1. In sentence 1, the word *deprivation* means
- A. oversupply.
- B. fear.
- C. loss.
- D. appreciation.

___ 2. In sentence 7, the word *diminished* means
- A. known.
- B. decreased.
- C. strengthened.
- D. defined.

___ 3. The main idea of this passage is expressed in sentence
- A. 1.
- B. 2.
- C. 6.
- D. 7.

___ 4. A night without sleep most affects your ability to answer
- A. multiple choice questions.
- B. true/false questions.
- C. essay questions.

___ 5. Lack of sleep most weakens
- A. memory.
- B. mental flexibility.
- C. familiar problem-solving techniques.

(Continues on next page)

___ 6. The relationship between sentences 2 and 3 is one of

A. addition.
B. time.
C. cause and effect.
D. contrast.

___ 7. The relationship of sentence 5 to sentences 2–4 is one of

A. addition.
B. time.
C. contrast.
D. illustration.

___ 8. We can infer from the passage that

A. teachers should not use essay questions.
B. too little sleep one night can harm one's health.
C. students get more sleep than other people.
D. too little sleep might weaken one's performance at work.

Name ______________________

Section ____________ Date __________

SCORE: (Number correct) × 12.5 = ______%

COMBINED SKILLS: Test B

After reading the passage, write the letter of the best answer to each question.

[1]One reason for listening is to help others with their problems. [2]One type of helpful response, the supporting response, can take several forms. [3]Sometimes it involves reassuring: "You've got nothing to worry about—I know you'll do a good job." [4]In other cases, support comes through comforting: "Don't worry. We all love you." [5]We can also support people in need by distracting them with humor, kidding, and joking.

[6]Sometimes a person simply needs encouragement, and in these cases a supporting response can be the best thing. [7]But in many instances this kind of comment isn't helpful at all; in fact, it can even make things worse. [8]Telling a person who is very upset that everything is all right or joking about what seems like a serious problem can communicate the idea that you don't think the problem is really worth all the fuss. [9]People might see your comments as a putdown, leaving them feeling worse than before.

___ 1. In sentence 3, the word *reassuring* means
- A. kidding.
- B. doubting.
- C. listening carefully.
- D. making confident.

___ 2. The main idea of the first paragraph of the passage is expressed in sentence
- A. 1.
- B. 2.
- C. 3.
- D. 5.

___ 3. Which sentence best expresses the implied main idea of the second paragraph?
- A. A supporting response can be the best thing in some cases.
- B. Supporting responses are not always helpful.
- C. People often need encouragement.
- D. A supporting response is rarely helpful.

___ 4. A supporting response can
- A. reassure.
- B. comfort.
- C. entertain.
- D. all of the above.

(Continues on next page)

___ 5. The relationship of sentence 5 to sentences 3 and 4 is one of
   A. time.
   B. addition.
   C. illustration.
   D. contrast.

___ 6. The relationship of sentence 7 to sentence 6 is one of
   A. comparison.
   B. contrast.
   C. addition.
   D. an example.

___ 7. The first paragraph
   A. describes steps in the process of how best to listen to others.
   B. lists forms of supporting responses.
   C. contrasts types of listeners.
   D. narrates a series of events about listening.

___ 8. The author implies that when trying to be helpful,
   A. we should rarely use humor.
   B. we must make a judgment about how to be helpful in each case.
   C. we can listen without responding.
   D. all of the above.

Name ______________________

Section ____________ Date ____________

SCORE: (Number correct) × 12.5 = ______%

COMBINED SKILLS: Test C

After reading the passage, write the letter of the best answer to each question.

[1]Say that you're interested in selling blue jeans in your community. [2]If your rival is selling blue jeans for $48 a pair, you might try attracting business by offering the jeans for $45. [3]The catch, of course, is that you'll get $3 less than your rival does for each pair you sell, and you'll still have to cover the same expenses—buying the jeans from the manufacturer, paying rent on your store, and so forth.

[4]How, then, can you charge less and still make a worthwhile profit? [5]The answer—you hope—is that the lower price will attract more customers. [6]Even though you make less money than your rival does on each pair of jeans, you'll sell more of them and so come out with a good overall profit.

[7]A business owner who can improve efficiency and reduce operating costs may be able to lower prices without settling for a smaller profit per unit. [8]If you are selling blue jeans, for example, you may find that installing a new lighting system cuts the electric bills. [9]You can maintain your profits at a lower selling price and pass the savings along to customers.

[10]Head-on competition like this tends to keep prices down, which is good for the buying public. [11]At the same time, it holds out the promise of great profits to the business that can sell more of its product or service than competitors do.

___ 1. In the first paragraph, the word *rival* means
- A. neighbor.
- B. competitor.
- C. customer.
- D. manufacturer.

___ 2. In sentence 10, the term *head-on* means
- A. unfair.
- B. rare.
- C. useless.
- D. direct.

___ 3. Which subject is the main topic of the passage?
- A. Head-on competition
- B. Blue jeans
- C. Electric bills
- D. Business expenses

(Continues on next page)

___ 4. Which sentence best expresses the main idea of the passage?
A. There is great competition in blue jeans sales.
B. A lower price attracts more customers.
C. Head-on competition tends to keep prices down for the public while holding out the promise of great profits to business owners.
D. There are several ways for business owners to keep prices down and still make a worthwhile profit.

___ 5. To charge less and still make a good profit, business owners can
A. sell more of a product.
B. cut costs.
C. both of the above.

___ 6. The relationship of sentence 8 to sentence 7 is one of
A. addition.
B. time.
C. illustration.
D. contrast.

___ 7. In the context of the passage, competition is a(n)
A. cause of business decisions.
B. part of a list of items.
C. new term being defined.
D. example.

___ 8. We might conclude from the passage that *without* competition,
A. the public would benefit from lower prices.
B. business owners would make lower profits.
C. business owners would have little reason to lower prices.
D. there would be more products.

Name ______________________________
Section ______________ Date ____________
SCORE: (Number correct) × 12.5 = ______%

COMBINED SKILLS: Test D

After reading the passage, write the letter of the best answer to each question.

[1]Business ethics is more complicated than it used to be. [2]Back in the "bad old days," in the early 1900s, the prevailing view among industrialists was that business had only one responsibility: to make a profit. [3]Railroad tycoon William Vanderbilt summed up this attitude when he said, "The public be damned. [4]I'm working for the shareholders."

[5]The beginning of the twentieth century was not a good time to be a low-level worker or a careless consumer. [6]For instance, people worked sixty-hour weeks under dreadful conditions for a dollar or two a day. [7]The few bold souls who tried to fight the system faced violence and unemployment. [8]Consumers were not much better off. [9]*Caveat emptor* was the rule of the day—"Let the buyer beware." [10]If you bought a product, you paid the price and took the consequences. [11]There were no consumer groups or government agencies to come to your defense if the product was defective or caused harm. [12]And if you tried to sue the company, chances were you would lose.

[13]These conditions caught the attention of a few crusading journalists known as muckrakers. [14]They used the power of the press to stir up public anger and desire for reform. [15]Largely through their efforts, a number of laws were passed to limit the power of monopolies and to establish safety standards for food and drugs.

___ 1. In sentence 2, the word *prevailing* means
A. unlikely.
B. friendly.
C. illegal.
D. widely accepted.

___ 2. In sentence 11, the word *defective* means
A. good.
B. faulty.
C. harmful.
D. old.

___ 3. The main idea of the second paragraph is expressed in sentence
A. 5.
B. 6.
C. 8.
D. 12.

___ 4. The muckrakers were
A. consumers.
B. journalists.
C. employers.
D. government agencies.

(Continues on next page)

___ 5. The author quotes Vanderbilt in order to make clear the early-twentieth-century attitude held by

A. workers.
B. heads of industry.
C. muckrakers.
D. consumers.

___ 6. The main pattern of organization of the second paragraph is

A. contrast.
B. definition and example.
C. list of items.
D. time order.

___ 7. The relationship of sentence 6 to sentence 5 is one of

A. addition.
B. time.
C. illustration.
D. contrast.

___ 8. The author implies that

A. consumers are better off today than they were at the beginning of the twentieth century.
B. journalism can greatly influence conditions in this country.
C. at the beginning of the twentieth century, employers sometimes used force to get their way.
D. all of the above.

ANSWERS TO THE TESTS IN THE TEST BANK

DICTIONARY USE: Test A

A. 1–2. easy, earthquake
3–4. glide, gloat
5–6. hide-out, hi-fi
7–8. rock 'n' roll, roger
9–10. Thursday, tiddlywinks

B. 11. occupation
12. cancer
13. error
14. military
15. mystery

C. 16. ten
17. she
18. card
19. up
20. use

DICTIONARY USE: Test B

1. mar•ket mär′kĭt
2. zip•per zĭp′ər
3. frac•ture frăk′chər
4. di•min•ish dĭ-mĭn′ĭsh
5. pes•ti•cide pĕs′tĭ-sīd′
6. invention, logic
7. logic
8. invention
9. moonstruck
10. logic, moonstruck
11. noun, verb
12. adj., verb, noun
13. adj., noun, pron.
14. prep., adv., adj.
15. verb, noun, adj.
16. volcanoes
17. families
18. halves
19. teeth
20. mice

DICTIONARY USE: Test C

A. 1. A
2. B
3. A
4. 3
5. 1
6. B
7. B
8. D
9. 2
10. 1

B. 11. season
12. believable
13. emergency
14. governor
15. indifferent

C. 16. nif•ty nĭf′tē
17. fru•gal fro͞o′gəl
18. for•feit fôr′fĭt
19. feath•er•brain fĕth′ər-brān′
20. ster•e•o•type stĕr′ē-ə-tīp′

DICTIONARY USE: Test D

A. 1. D
2. B
3. D
4. A
5. A
6. A
7. B
8. A
9. B
10. E

B. 11. heroes
12. cities
13. calves
14. sisters-in-law

C. *(Wording of definitions may vary.)*
15–16. pär′shəl; having a particular liking or fondness for
17–18. sănd′băgd; treat severely or unjustly
19–20. tām; not exciting, dull, flat

VOCABULARY IN CONTEXT: Test A

A. 1. Examples: *vegetables and herbs from China, spices from India, olives from Greece, cheeses from France;* D
2. Examples: *washing dishes for hours, flipping burgers day after day;* C
3. Examples: *suicide, murder;* C

B. 4. overjoyed
5. ceremonies

C. 6. Antonym: *slow down;* D
7. Antonym: *deny;* B

D. 8. B
9. A
10. A

VOCABULARY IN CONTEXT: Test B

A. 1. Examples: *bad news in every letter, an F on every test, a "no" to every request;* C
2. *someone was plotting against him, he was being controlled by something put into his brain;* B

B. 3. twist
4. strengthen
5. supporter

C. 6. Antonym: *unnoticeable*; B
7. Antonym: *simple;* D
8. Antonym: *expert;* C

D. 9. C
10. A

VOCABULARY IN CONTEXT: Test C

1. A
2. C
3. D
4. B
5. A
6. C
7. D
8. D
9. B
10. C

VOCABULARY IN CONTEXT: Test D

1. A
2. D
3. D
4. C
5. B
6. B
7. D
8. B
9. B
10. C

MAIN IDEAS: Test A

A. 1. TV program
2. flavor
3. fastener
4. entertainer
5. family
6. emotion
7. road

Items 8–15: Answers will vary. Examples are given.

B. 8. leaking toilet, roaches
9. train, car
10. peach, plum
11. beagle, poodle
12. Christmas, birthday
13. Spanish, Italian
14. what, when
15. buy a home, own a small business

Items 16–25: Specific ideas may vary;examples are given.

C.16. punishment, jail term
17. sweetener, sugar
18. body of water, ocean
19. exercise, jogging
20. chore, taking out garbage
21. medicine, aspirin
22. difficult weather, blizzard
23. wood, pine
24. seasoning, salt
25. symptom, fever

MAIN IDEAS: Test B

A. 1. book
2. flower
3. bedding
4. expense
5. reptile
6. joint
7. gas
8. writer

B.

Group 1	*Group 2*	*Group 3*
S	S	P
P	S	S
S	P	S
S	S	S

MAIN IDEAS: Test C

Items 1–6: Specific ideas may vary. Examples are given.

A. 1. fish, salmon
2. amount, ounce
3. outerwear, overcoat
4. dairy product, cheese
5. furniture, chair
6. fictional character, Scrooge

B. S
S
P
S

C.

Group 1	*Group 2*
SD	T
MI	SD
T	SD
SD	MI

D. 19. B
20. C

MAIN IDEAS: Test D

A. 1. T
2. SD
3. SD
4. MI

B. 5. B
6. Sentence 1
7. C
8. Sentence 5
9. A
10. Sentence 3

SUPPORTING DETAILS: Test A

Wording of answers may vary.

A. (1–5.) 1. Provide a stimulating environment.
2. Focus on the child's strengths.
4. Set an example in your choices of work or hobbies.
5. Do not use rigid control.

5. ways *or* ways in which parents can encourage creativity in children

B. (6–10.) *Heading:* . . . influence people's eating habits.

Culture Economics

9. Another
10. third

SUPPORTING DETAILS: Test B

Wording of answers may vary slightly.

A. (1–4.) 1. Autocratic leader
2. Democratic leader—shares authority
3. "Hands off" leader—takes the role of a consultant

4. three broad types *or* three broad types of leadership

B. (5–10.)

Special interest groups	Public interest groups—pursue benefits for society
[Examples:] Chambers of commerce, trade associations, labor unions, farm organizations	*Examples:* Consumer protection organizations

9. One
10. second

SUPPORTING DETAILS: Test C

Wording of answers may vary.

A. (1–6.) 1. . . . you know about and are interested in.
2. Prepare well.
   a. Organize your points.
   b. Rehearse your speech several times.
3. Practice relaxation activities just before your speech.
   a. Clear your mind.

B. (7–10.) *Heading:* . . . keep the demands of home and job in balance.

Set limits. | List things to do in order of importance. | Don't aim for perfection.

SUPPORTING DETAILS: Test D

Wording of answers may vary.

A. (1–6.) 1. b. . . . multiply and spread.
2. a. Disease is highly contagious.
4. Decline stage
   b. Sometimes you can transmit the disease to others.
5. Convalescence
   b. Most diseases are not contagious during this stage.

B. (7–10.)

Passive behavior | Aggressive behavior | Assertive behavior

Aggressive behavior: Lash out at those who hurt them.

LOCATIONS OF MAIN IDEAS: Test A

1. 5
2. 1
3. 2
4. 2
5. 1

LOCATIONS OF MAIN IDEAS: Test B

1. 1
2. 3
3. 6
4. 1
5. 2

LOCATIONS OF MAIN IDEAS: Test C

1. 8
2. 1
3. 1
4. 1
5. 3

LOCATIONS OF MAIN IDEAS: Test D

1. 1
2. 1
3. 3
4. 6
5. 3

RELATIONSHIPS I: Test A

A. 1. E later
2. C First
3. D In addition
4. B Another
5. A after

B. 6. One
7. after
8. second
9. Finally
10. A

RELATIONSHIPS I: Test B

A. 1. B
2. B
3. A
4. B
5. A

B. 6. A

C. 7. During
8. next
9. final
10. B

RELATIONSHIPS I: Test C

A. 1. A
2–3. *Any two of these:* first, second, third

B. 4. B
5. next

C. 6. A

Wording of outline answers may vary.

7–10. *Heading:* . . . types of listening.
1. Appreciative listening
3. Comprehensive listening—to understand the message of a speaker
4. Critical listening

RELATIONSHIPS I: Test D

A. 1. A
2. 3
3. final

B. 4. A
5–6. *Any two of these:* For one thing, Also, Last

C. 7. B

Wording of map answers may vary.

8–10. *Heading:* . . . the product life cycle.
2. Growth stage: Rapid jump in sales; competition increases; war for market share begins
4. Decline stage: Sales and profits slip and fade away

RELATIONSHIPS II: Test A

A. 1. C differently
2. E In contrast
3. A As a result
4. D For example
5. B Because of

B. 6. C
7. A
8. C
9. A
10. B

RELATIONSHIPS II: Test B

A. 1. C
2. But *or* On the other hand

B. 3. A
4. example

C. 5. B
6. reason *or* causes

D. 7. C
8. differ *or* However

E. 9. B
10. effects *or* caused *or* As a result *or* causing

RELATIONSHIPS II: Test C

A. 1. A
2. B
3. result in *or* led to

B. 4–5. B, C

C. 6. C

7–10.

Interpersonal *setting*

Informal *language*

When talking with our best friend

When talking with strangers

RELATIONSHIPS II: Test D

A. 1. B

Wording of outline answers may vary slightly.

2–5. *Main idea:* Fatigue . . .

1. b. From using muscles that have not been used for a while
2. a. Poisons from disease-causing agents get into the bloodstream
5. Boredom

B. 6. A
7. A

Wording of map answers may vary.

8–10.

Middle managers—develop plans to carry out top managers' goals

First-line managers—oversee employees; put into action plans developed at higher levels

Examples: foreman, department head, office manager

INFERENCES: Test A

1. B, C
2. B, D
3. B, C
4. B, D
5. A, D

INFERENCES: Test B

1. A, D
2. B, C
3. B, C, D
4. A, D, E

INFERENCES: Test C

A. 2, 3
B. 1, 4, 5
C. 2, 6, 7, 9, 10

INFERENCES: Test D

A. 1, 3, 6, 7, 10
B. 2, 3, 4, 7, 10

IMPLIED MAIN IDEAS: Test A

A. 1. C
2. C
3. B
4. A
5. A
6. A
7. A
8. B

B. 9. *(Group 1)* B
10. *(Group 2)* C

IMPLIED MAIN IDEAS: Test B

Wording of answers may vary.

A. 1. Ways to cook eggs
2. Floor coverings
3. Preparation for grocery shopping
4. Sources of heat
5. Steps in writing a paper
6. Endings
7. Things with stripes
8. Things people fear

B. 9. B
10. C

IMPLIED MAIN IDEAS: Test C

1. D
2. D
3. C
4. B
5. A

IMPLIED MAIN IDEAS: Test D

1. B
2. C
3. D
4. C
5. A

THE BASICS OF ARGUMENT: Test A

A. 1. S
2. S
3. S
4. P
5. S
6. S
7. P
8. S

B. 9. B

C. 10. B

THE BASICS OF ARGUMENT: Test B

1–3. A, B, D
4–6. B, C, D
7–9. A, C, E
10. B

THE BASICS OF ARGUMENT: Test C

A. 1. S
2. S
3. P
4. S

B. 5. B
6. C
7–9. B, C, D
10. C

THE BASICS OF ARGUMENT: Test D

A. 1. S
2. P
3. S
4. S

B. 5. A

C. 6–8. B, C, E

D. 9. Group 1: C
10. Group 2: C

COMBINED SKILLS: Test A

1. C
2. B
3. A
4. C
5. B
6. C
7. C
8. D

COMBINED SKILLS: Test B

1. D
2. B
3. B
4. D
5. B
6. B
7. B
8. B

COMBINED SKILLS: Test C

1. B
2. D
3. A
4. C
5. C
6. C
7. A
8. C

COMBINED SKILLS: Test D

1. D
2. B
3. A
4. B
5. B
6. C
7. C
8. D

Notes